What People are Saying
About *Violated Online*™

"Steven Wyer nails it. The book is not just a list of dangers, it's a plan of action. If you don't control your online image, someone else will."

—**Trevor Matich,** ESPN Football Analyst

"A practical how-to-guide for everyone concerned about protecting his or her online reputation or company brand. A must read because credibility matters in life and in business."

—**Kathleen Calligan,** CEO, Better Business Bureau Middle Tennessee

"Every business involved in the capital markets is exposed by uncontrollable online information. Online reputation management is vital for private and public companies, officers, directors and senior management. It is about time a book like this was written."

—**J. Ramson,** Pro-Active Capital Resources Group

"'...he that filches from me my good name robs me... and makes me poor indeed.' Shakespeare never heard of the Internet, but Steven Wyer's book warns us that today's technology makes us more vulnerable to the theft of reputation than when the Bard put the words into the mouth of the villainous Iago. And, Wyer informs us that we have ways and weapons to protect against the robbery that can 'make us poor indeed.'"

—**John Seigenthaler,** Founder, First Amendment Center, Vanderbilt University & Founding Editorial Director of *USA Today*

"There are few things more hurtful and frustrating in life as to become a victim of anonymous slander posted on the Internet for the whole world to see. I know this from first-hand experience and, even as a public figure, have found it very difficult to fight back against some of the most over-the-top defamatory outrages imaginable. Violated Online is a great and much-needed guide for anyone and everyone — from the celebrity to the most private person — because, like it or not, we are all potential victims in the 21st century."

— **Joseph Farah,** Editor and CEO, WND.com and WND Books

violated™
ONLINE

IF YOU THINK YOU ARE SAFE...THINK AGAIN.

How Online Slander Can Destroy Your Life
and What You Must Do to Protect Yourself

Steven Wyer

with Jeremy Dunlap

Published in Nashville, Tennessee
by Dunham Books, 63 Music Square East, Nashville, TN 37203.

The nature of our work requires both trust and discretion. For this reason, all of the names and geographic locations that are mentioned in this book have been changed. The material facts for each story are absolutely true. You cannot easily make this stuff up.

Disclaimer: This book is not intended as a substitute for legal or Search Engine Reputation Management advice. The specific facts that apply to your matter may make the outcome different than would be anticipated by you.

ISBN 978-0-9837456-0-0

Printed in the United States of America
11 12 13 14   5 4 3 2 1

This book is dedicated to my

Uncle Keith (Poobah) Gibson,

the wisest man I know.

He taught me to remember that

If it's not one thing,

it's another.

Table of Contents

I must confess that I've never trusted the Web.

I've always seen it as a coward's tool.

Where does it live? How do you hold it personally responsible?

Can you put a distributed network of fiber-optic cable "on notice?"

And is it male or female?

In other words, can I challenge it to a fight?

— **Stephen Colbert**

Preface

I grew up believing the playing field of life was pretty fair; maybe you did, too. If two people had a disagreement, it could be worked out. If a person was slandered, there was recourse through the courts where justice would be served up fairly. But the playing field of the past has been paved over. It is now an information super highway—a highway that covers the globe. *All of it.* It's difficult to process the speed with which things have changed. The rules for playing are different now, and we don't know what to do about it.

I talk to people all the time that say things like, "I don't do the Internet" or, "social media is for kids." I used to think these people were just too lazy to learn something new but don't believe that anymore. I've come to realize that mostly they are just plain scared. They know enough to understand that there is danger out there, but they are not sure exactly *what* is dangerous or what to *do* about the danger. I hope this book helps.

Recently, a friend made a comment on my Facebook page. I'd posted a link to an article that announced the White House had added a new position to deal with online media. The post, within its communications department, is titled "Director of Progressive Media & Online Response." (Our tax dollars at work).

And you don't think every other sitting President had the same kind of media management? my friend asked. My answer was simple. *No.*

While politicians have always had influence over the media, the tables have turned and people now have a way to express themselves through digital media that cannot be easily stifled. The people have a voice and it can be used for good. This ability has never been available in the history of our planet.

But for every good thing, there is a shadow side. While the White House has ample resources in the form of our tax dollars to deploy in defense of the sitting president, the majority of citizens do not. And in fact, most of those that *do* have the resources don't know how to use them to protect themselves.

A cardiologist is criminally charged with sexual misconduct. He is arrested, booked and formally charged. The medical partnership he practices with asks for his resignation. The media eat him up, his family is humiliated and his thirty-year career is destroyed. The doctor is found completely innocent by a jury, and it is disclosed that the person who filed the suit had perpetrated the same smear tactic ten years prior on another doctor. The court expunges his record and no evidence of the nightmare exists—except online. The news stories remain; the blogs that take cheap shots still show up when his name is searched. Everything is there, and it will be for twenty years. The doctor finally decides to change vocations.

People often ask how I found my way into Search Engine Reputation Management (SERM), and it is a fair question. The direct answer is that I was involved in a lawsuit. While I used to live by the belief that we are innocent until proven guilty, I learned the hard way it doesn't work like that anymore. The online accusations damaged my business, hurt my family and deeply affected my income. And if it can happen to me, it can happen to you.

Since then, I have personally talked to hundreds of people with stories woven from the shadow side of the Internet. Their narratives would sound like fiction, were it not for the fact that I have helped many of them reclaim their lives and their dignity. The shadows exist for professionals, college students, small businesses and public companies. We are not talking about a small group of people on the fringe; we are talking about literally millions of people—people just like you and me.

As you will read, our government has passed laws that, in attempting to support the right to free speech, leave its citizens open to be maligned with impunity by accusers both real and fictitious. Our basic rights to privacy are being run over by data aggregators, cookies on our computers and profiteers that cash in on our suffering. I have sadly come to the conclusion that there is no one out there who is going to protect us. We have to do this ourselves.

My hope is that in reading the stories of others, you will come to understand the dangers lurking "out there," and the defenses you will need to survive. *Being aware* is the beginning of *being prepared*. Being prepared will empower you to take action and your actions will protect you from being *Violated Online.*

Congress shall make no law respecting an establishment of religion, or prohibiting the free exercise thereof; or abridging the freedom of speech, or of the press; or the right of the people peaceably to assemble, and to petition the Government for a redress of grievances.

**—The First Amendment
to the United States Constitution**

Chapter 1
Violated Out of Nowhere:
When Did This Happen?

Sometimes history happens when nobody is looking.

It's the most common question we hear when people call us about their online reputation. *How and when did this happen?* The focus on day-to-day business and a general lack of understanding about the over-arching power of Google, Yahoo! and Bing's search results has brought about *The Perfect Storm.* Perhaps you have heard this film title used to describe various situations in life. As one reviewer laid out the plot...

> *In the fall of 1991, the Andrea Gail left Gloucester, Mass. and headed for the fishing grounds of the North Atlantic. Two weeks later, an event took place that had never occurred in recorded history.*[1]

In this movie, a sea captain played by George Clooney was involved in a highly competitive business and had been stung by a string of missed income projections. His crew had barely arrived back in port when he told them he was going out again, even though it was the time of year when the weather often turned ugly. Neglecting to pay attention to the weather reports fostered an ignorance that kept him in the dark regarding a world-class storm on the way that could potentially kill him, his crew and his competition. However, unlike George Clooney's character, his competitors did become aware of the oncoming storm and headed for shelter. If you haven't seen the movie it is worth a click to Netflix.

Five years after this blockbuster film hit theatres, another "perfect storm" began to take shape. Few suspected that the Communications Decency Act of 1996 and the Digital Copyright Act of 1998 would change our world forever. A lack of attention to the news fostered an ignorance that kept most people in the dark regarding the world-class storm brewing—a tempest that could potentially kill them, their vocations and their futures. This modern day parallel is a good beginning for an answer to the questions of *how?* and *when?*

It all began on September 4, 1998, when two PhD students at Stanford University started a company now known throughout the planet as Google. They found humor in the name *Google*, which had its origin in the word *googol*, a term for the number that represents "one followed by a hundred zeros."[2] Turns out the hundred zeros foreshadowed what is now the largest single source of information aggregation in history. With more than one trillion pages of content and availability in about 130 different languages, there is nowhere in the civilized world where a person cannot access Google's endless deluge of information. When you combine this reach—a massive tsunami of information available to nearly every human being alive—with the emergence of social networks, online conditions rapidly change.

It's difficult to remember the world, pre-Facebook. Yet prior to Facebook was Myspace, and before MySpace, Friendster. *Who remembers Friendster?* Not many, even though Friendster, founded in 2002 by Jonathan Abrams and Peter Chin, was the conceptual pioneer in social networking sites. Abrams, a former Netscape employee, began mulling over a software idea *where people somehow could integrate online and offline identities.* Sound familiar?

The Friendster experiment, backed by major venture capital dollars, built a momentum of three million users in just a short time. Overnight, Abrams became a celebrity, appearing on late night talk shows and having his picture show up on magazine covers. In 2003, *Fortune* magazine wrote:

There may be a new kind of Internet emerging—one more about connecting people to people than people to websites.[3]

Can you hear the roar and growl of another wave in this storm beginning to build? In that same year, Friendster caught the attention of several companies, including Google, who would offer them a whopping $30 million dollar buyout. Friendster declined. In many ways, the rest is history. So what happened to the pioneering social networking website that should have changed the world? Well, Abrams did in fact change the world. His ideas were the catalyst for Myspace.

In August 2003, after the launch of Friendster the year before, several eUniverse employees with Friendster accounts realized its potential and decided to mimic the more popular features of the social networking website. Within ten days the first version of MySpace was ready for launch. A complete infrastructure of finance, human resources, technical expertise, bandwidth and server capacity was available for the new website, right out of the gate.[4] In 2006, MySpace was valued at hundreds of millions of dollars and registered its 100 millionth account[5]. By 2007, one in five Americans was visiting MySpace (while Friendster fell to 13th).[6] MySpace became *the place* for music, video, messaging, connecting and posting. However, there was another storm brewing within that perfect storm—Facebook.

By now, nearly every moviegoer has seen *The Social Network,* a 2011 Academy Award-winning movie about the humble beginnings of Facebook. But just in case you have no idea what I'm talking about, here is a summary of the event that changed the world. Facebook evolved from a simple concept that was initially limited to Harvard students and then opened up to other colleges in the Boston area, Ivy League schools and Stanford Univeristy. It later included all college students, expanded further to embrace high school students, and finally anyone over the age of 13. At the writing of this book, Facebook has passed 750 million active users worldwide. And according to ConsumersReports.org, in May 2011 there were 7.5 million children under 13 with accounts, *violating Facebook's own terms and conditions.*[7] While you might imagine a couple of brilliant students sitting for hours at a white board running complex calculations, evaluating the World Wide Web's potential and thinking great thoughts, here is what *really* happened.[8]

Harvard sophomore Mark Zuckerberg invented Facebook in his dorm room. Initially, Zuckerberg created Facemash, a Harvard University version of *Hot or Not*, according to school newspaper *The Harvard Crimson.*[9] On October 28, 2003, Zuckerberg was blogging about a girl who had dumped him and trying to think of something to do to get her off his mind.

I'm a little intoxicated, not gonna lie. So what if it's not even 10 p.m. and it's a Tuesday night? What? The Kirkland [dorm] facebook is open on my desktop and some of these people have pretty horrendous facebook pics. I almost want to put some of these faces next to pictures of farm animals and have people vote on which is more attractive. —9:48 pm

Yeah, it's on. I'm not exactly sure how the farm animals are going to fit into this whole thing (you can't really ever be sure with farm animals . . .), but I like the idea of comparing two people together. —11:09 pm

Let the hacking begin. —12:58 am

According to *The Harvard Crimson*, Facemash "used photos compiled from the online facebooks of nine Houses, placing two next to each other at a time and asking users to choose the 'hotter' person." To accomplish this, Zuckerberg hacked into protected areas of Harvard's computer network and copied the houses' private dormitory ID images. Harvard at that time did not have a student directory with photos and basic information, and the initial site generated 450 visitors and 22,000 photo-views in its first four hours online. The initial site mirrored people's physical community—with their real identities—and represented the key aspects of what would later become Facebook.[10]

By April 2008, according to Alexa website traffic rankings, Facebook overtook Myspace in the rankings bid. By February 2011, Myspace's website traffic ranking fell to number 56 as Facebook held position number two.[11] (Ironically, as I browsed an *Inc.* Magazine article online about the social networking site Friendster, I noticed a Facebook widget indicating that over 28,000 people "liked" their magazine.) With Goldman-Sachs now estimating a value of $50 billion dollars and private pre-IPO shares trading at levels suggesting a $100 billion dollar evaluation, Facebook's social networking empire has so impacted society that it now has its own social vernacular—"friend," as in *to friend someone*. Yes, Facebook is globally omnipresent.

This period of social media creation that includes blogging, wiki and video sharing sites has been dubbed Web 2.0. To explain what is meant by this, if Web 1.0 is simply reading words on a static Internet browser screen, then Web 2.0 is the ability to interact and collaborate, via the Internet, in a social dialogue. In 1999, just one year after Google was born, a forward thinking electronic information consultant named Darcy DiNucci wrote the following in an article entitled "Fragmented Future:"

*The Web we know now, which loads into a browser window in essentially static screenfulls, is only an embryo of the Web to come. The first glimmerings of Web 2.0 are beginning to appear, and we are just starting to see how that embryo might develop. The Web will be understood not as screenfulls of text and graphics but as **a transport mechanism**, the ether through which interactivity happens. It will...appear on your computer screen...on your TV set...on your car dashboard... your cell phone...hand-held game machines...**maybe even your microwave oven.**[12]*

So, from this brief history of federal government regulations, Google, Abram's Friendster and Zuckerberg's Facebook, we can begin to see a setting for *the perfect storm*. This was a window of time where young academics changed the world and never told us. While many middle school kids might have seen a storm brewing, the rest of us were just too busy trying to make a living. And fifteen years later, like it or not, our reality has changed forever. The tempest, however, is far from over. In fact, the storm of change is really just beginning. Many business owners who did not see this coming now feel as though their business is a little sailboat trying to stay afloat in the ocean of the World Wide Web. But there is another piece to this puzzle and it helps to answer our initial question: *How and when did all of this happen?*

The second component is paralleled in the nightmare that was my ninth grade year of high school—algebra. I struggled for months to master the concept of exponential growth—how money earning an interest rate of x, if left untouched, would compound for y number of years and reflect exponential growth. I nearly failed ninth grade algebra but *did* get the concept. While much of what I learned proved to be of little use in later vocations, the exponential growth concept is infinitely applicable to our perfect storm.

Social networks like Facebook have covered the globe as its members have compounded over time. In early 2011, accumulated membership surpassed the number of citizens in Japan. Facebook's subscriber base swelled to a number that was greater than the population of the United States—every man, woman and child—multiplied times two!

In July 2006, social networkers were introduced to a new social site with an odd name. The exponential growth of this site, Twitter, is reported to have equaled a monthly expansion of 1,382 percent. Not only that, but most of the site's users are older adults who might not have used other social sites before Twitter.[13] That is some serious exponential growth, and according to Twitter they have just begun! Twitter's projections for the end of 2013—$1.54 billion in revenue, $111 million in net earnings, and *one billion users*. A billion users in just seven years! Stop and get your head around *that*.

So there is our perfect storm—the emergence of global-reaching search engines, the creation of three huge social networks fueled by venture capital, very smart people, and waves of exponential growth that continue to grow larger and stronger. Much of our culture now has the hang of social networking, how it works and how to use it—meaning that things continue to move even faster. Exponential growth is taking place.

Since 2008, there has been a massive tsunami of virtual information. The storm front has now moved from personal computers and transportable laptops to smart phones, netbooks, iPads and even digital watches. In short, at any given moment, there is limitless information on every topic known to humankind right at our fingertips—including information about *you*.

With just a few clicks anyone can access multiple bits of information about you, including your physical mailing address, phone numbers, your travel calendar, the number of kids you have, pictures you have posted, previous arrest records or legal infractions, unpaid taxes, political campaign contributions—even pieces of your social security number.

And I am just getting started.

While someone—a former employee, an ex-lover, or a friend—is viewing that information about you, they can create additional information, be it fact or fiction; *whatever they choose.* Think about it. What could they write about you and repost numerous times without your knowledge—with little legal recourse available to you? And by the way, whatever they could or would write wouldn't even have to be truthful! We'll have more to say about *that* in the remaining chapters of the book.

While at times, with cause, we read headlines and worry about the Federal Trade Commission attempting to regulate blogging,[14] the Federal Communications Commission ideas on net neutrality, or that Google and the National Security Agency have allegedly been working on surveillance of American citizens, maybe the *real* worry for you should be the person sitting next to you on the bus, at lunch, coffee, in traffic, or at the office. Freaked out? You might be. Are you feeling small, swallowed up or lacking control? If you are, that is completely normal. Should you be feeling violated? *Definitely.*

Referring back to our opening story, it is not too late to examine the "weather reports" about this raging storm. In *The Perfect Storm,* Captain Billy Tyne had ignored all the warning signs before blindly casting off on his final voyage. As the film concludes, Captain Tyne is crushed by the waves, knocked out of the boat and drowned. However, the conclusion to the perfect storm raging around you *can* be different. But just as ignorance did not keep Captain Tyne safe, ignorance will not keep you safe, either.

My hope is that this book will serve as a weather report to educate and empower you to take control of your online reputation. It is time to understand that what you place on the Internet—or what is being placed about you on the Internet—is viewable by the whole world. And while you cannot control the raging storm of the World Wide Web anymore than Captain Tyne could prevent the perfect storm, you *can* be prepared for when you are *Violated Online.*

Five Things to Remember

1. Ignorance is not a solution.

2. Our culture has completely adopted
interactive digital media.

3. Linear progression happens.

4. Interactive digital mediums are progressing faster than
we can really understand.

5. You must get involved and begin reading the weather reports *now,*
before the storm.

Chapter 2
Violated by Transparency

One person's transparency is another person's shame.

Wanda was on long-term sick leave for depression. Then her employer's insurance agent found photos on a popular social networking site that showed her having a good time at a Chippendale bar show, at her birthday party and on a summer holiday. According to the agent, this evidence proved that she was no longer depressed. Wanda is now fighting to have her benefits reinstated after her employer's insurance company cut them off.

Oops.

Whether or not she was suffering from depression or defrauded the insurance company is not germane to our discussion. What *is* relevant is how this incident has affected online search results delivered for her name. When she *"googles"* herself now, there are pages of allegations about her defrauding an insurance company. Some search results tell the story in great detail and are embellished with plenty of rude comments from readers belittling her intelligence. A search of her name delivers posting after posting of a now infamous Facebook picture of Wanda on the beach. So what will happen down the road when she interviews for another job and the employer—as most do today—does a simple search on her name? Do you really think Wanda will get the job? Certainly, Wanda's world has been changed in ways that she never dreamed of 4000 days ago, for now her whole life is a resume.

Did you catch that? *Your whole life is now an online resume*—an open book.

Historically, your personal biography and business resume were developed over time. By reading, editing and asking others for input, you were able to fine-tune your introduction to a prospective employer. Times have changed. Today your whole life, thanks to the Internet and social media, is now a resume. Your public self is exactly that. It is what is seen in the virtual public eye. And your public self reflects not only the *actual* you, but the *perceived* public image of you. Now stop and think about what you have placed in front of the virtual world. Have you taken care before providing that information?

It is said that for every *yin* there is a *yang* and that holds true for the Internet, too. Today, when kids need answers to their questions, they turn to doing research on the Internet. The *yin* side of the Internet is the power for good in education, medicine, human rights, third world development and global understanding. It allows this and future generations to understand life and business in a more comprehensive way than Childcraft or Encyclopedia Britannica ever allowed for me.

Then there is the *yang* and that is what this book is about. It's the shadow side of the Internet. Recently, a colleague asked if I worried that this book would show people how to slander others online. He was shocked by my answer. *There are already websites instructing readers how to slander people online.* The Internet recently allowed two Lee County, Florida teenage girls to allegedly produce a fake Facebook profile in the name of a classmate and post fake photographs of their victim simply because they thought it "would be funny."[15]

The stories in this book provide vivid details of the shadow side of the Internet—content, comments, social sites exposing individual convictions and slander that has come from the most unexpected places. In a moment we will define "online slander," but first I want to make the following suggestion: *You can be your own worst enemy when it comes to your online identity.*

Social networking sites such as Twitter, Facebook, LinkedIn and dozens of others offer the ability to publish interests, locations, work history, relationships, birthdates, GPS real-time locations and more. When social sites are developed, the goal is to provide a simple, intuitive user experience. But this process also allows personal information to be gathered, retained and evaluated, and then utilized to present you with "opportunities." When you volunteer that information, you may believe that it's simply stored for convenience. (That's what digital cookies are for, right?) But convenience probably has very little to do with it. And although receiving dozens of birthday greetings online is flattering, it may be good to consider what else can be done with those dates, addresses, phone numbers and other sensitive data. (While this book deals with online violations, may I offer one side note? *Many times an "offline" violation is made easier by what has been posted online.*)

This new reality of *your life is a resume* requires a discipline not often considered by most business people. Spontaneity can deliver much more harm than is understood on the front side of the mouse click. Five years ago, the primary online concern of most business people before hitting the send button was to make sure that the person named in the "To" field of an email was indeed the intended recipient before they hit the send button. Going back even further, I remember the days of filling out a credit card application with a pencil first to ensure I got accurate information in each field before I traced over the information with an ink pen. How times have changed!

Social media, coupled with a misguided sense of anonymity, places us in a vortex where we may reveal more in an instant than we would otherwise consider, given pen and paper. Whether it is a false sense of security sitting behind a computer at home or a dangerous comfort level with unfamiliar technology, many individuals—maybe you?— have given little thought to posting the most intimate details about personal lives, history, opinions, family, or business.

Then there are sites like Spokeo.com that pull information from multiple sources. At the time of publication, this little website in the wrong hands has the potential to cause you great anguish. Spokeo claims to gather personal information that can include credit scores, household income, religious preferences and much, much more. And get this: Spokeo, while searching *another person independent of you*, can include in its search results information about and posts written by you, simply because you were on the other person's "friend list."

The Spokeo "Friends" tab allows an individual, with whom you have—or once had—a relationship, to access information about you by searching their email address book. *Not good!* For a small fee, Spokeo will allow your current and/or former friend, according to the website, to *scan email contacts to discover surprising facts about your friends.* Right above that statement are the words: *Uncover personal photos, videos and blogs....*

I tried it. Once I entered an email account, Spokeo began the process of loading my address book, and from there it started searching for my friends, pulling information from the following sites:

- YouTube
- Webshots
- Digg
- Facebook
- Multiply
- Veoh
- Picturetrail
- MySpace

- LinkedIn
- Netlog
- Slide
- Flickr
- Fotolog

- hi5
- Bebo
- Amazon
- StumbleUpon

Can you see where this leads?

Before continuing, let's stop for a minute and establish a working definition of "online slander":

Communication (for written, broadcast, or otherwise published words) of a statement that makes a claim, expressly stated or implied to be factual, that may give an individual, business, product or group a negative image. It is usually a requirement that the claim be false and acknowledges that the online slander is communicated to someone other than the person defamed.

Have you ever offered a review on Amazon? Ever commented on LinkedIn, MySpace, or Facebook? Can you imagine if something you posted in haste like a photo, blog comment, or a book review could be found and easily misinterpreted—or edited to suit a slanderous intention? What kind of *claim, expressly stated or implied to be factual, that might give an individual, business, product or group a negative image* could be written based upon your postings? What hurt and damage could that cause? Welcome to the *yang*.

To help you begin dealing with the shadow side of the Internet, there are three questions that need to be asked by you...*about yourself.* The first question deals with the information that is already available when your name is searched. It will help you build a framework from which to function when you are logged online.

Question #1: How much transparency is too much transparency?

In the 2008 best-selling book, *Radically Transparent,*[16] authors Andy Beal and Dr. Judy Strauss offer insights into how best to navigate the issues of managing and monitoring your reputation online. They make an extremely relevant point to the topic at hand:

> *There is little censorship in the world of online social media— the community values raw truth. The Internet community immediately comes down hard on those who employ conversation spin, control, manipulation or spam. Anonymity is discouraged, and nearly all posts to a conversation include the author's real identity. On this new playing field, you need to be authentic or someone will discover the truth and you'll be exposed to millions.*

The concept of *little censorship* leaves no doubt that untruths, aspersions and slander about you can be placed on the Internet with few repercussions. While *anonymity is discouraged,* negative content can easily be posted under an assumed or phantom name; you can be attacked by "Mickey Mouse" or "George Washington." At the end of the day, it is in your best interests to have whatever is revealed about you online be the truth instead of fictitious, malicious or deceptive. And while it may be true that once content is placed on the Internet it is rarely edited, altered, manipulated or removed, influence over how information is presented is a concept that warrants consideration. We will talk more about this later on.

As I have already pointed out, nearly every good deed or bad experience in your life might now be found with the click of a mouse. Education, personal, public, professional and family is all right there and it is your life! This form of transparency is almost unavoidable. But what about intentional transparency?

Let me make it clear that when I say *intentional transparency*, I'm not suggesting that you admit every mistake you ever made, or that every disagreement, failure, domestic dispute or unsatisfied customer should show up on the first page of your search results. However, *intentional transparency* means that *you* determine what kind of information is presented about you, your business, or your life. If indeed your whole life is your resume, then the concept of putting your best foot forward still exists. You have a "public self" that can be developed, fleshed-out and presented very intentionally.

If you are familiar and comfortable with the tools that can be utilized to develop your online identity, then through careful crafting of content, images and video you can be intentionally honest, transparent and forthright. If you are unsure, as many are, then there are professionals who will work on your behalf. Regardless, if someone has placed damaging content online about you or your business, don't fire off an angry letter or post a quick rebuttal. There is a significant difference between reacting and responding. A measured and thoughtful approach to any attack is what increases the likelihood that you will recover.

Question #2: What lines do you need to draw that you (your family/ business) will not cross when it comes to posting information online?

You must decide what you will *not* place on the Internet. This is true for you, your family members and your employees. Many companies now have a formal social media policy that spells out who can post content and where it can be placed. As a personal example, I am cautious about placing pictures of my family online. Remember Wanda? She had never taken the time to draw boundaries concerning what she would and would not post. Therefore, her only rule concerning posting material online was that there were no rules. I suggest coming up with a list of boundaries by asking some basic questions:

- Will we (as a family) instantly post pictures from our phones to social sites?
- What email address(es) and phone number(s) do we want to provide for public profile sites?
- Will we provide birth date/birth place information?
- If we own a business, should any employee be able to post content and rebuttals on the company website?
- Are the dates on my resumes and biographies accurate?
- What digital images should be posted and where?

Question #3: How deliberate should I be about offering opinions and comments (before they are online)?

Regarding timely deliberation before posting online, I offer this advice from my uncle, the wisest man I have ever known. Unk suggested, "When there is an important decision to make or trauma to deal with, give it three days before finalizing a decision," because "even Jesus took three days."

I've modified his three-day guideline into a self-imposed *24-hour rule*. It is amazing how often something can seem great in the moment of its creation but how poorly it reads just one day later. If there is any truth in my uncle's advice, then I suggest that there should be even more consideration given to what is posted online. Save your thoughts to a document or send an email to yourself and walk away for a bit. Later, referring to your established boundaries, return to reread the material with the following options:

- Edit the content,
- Post content as is, or
- Breathe a sigh of relief as you hit the delete button.

While some information can be edited once it is posted online, much cannot. If Wanda had just taken some time to breathe, found a bit of sobriety and let more rational thoughts prevail before posting, she would not have been dealing with such regret.

Better slow than sorry.

Five Things to Remember

1. Your life is a resume. Own it.

2. Be deliberate, methodical and measured when providing information online.

3. Set specific information boundaries.

4. Data aggregation delivers a comprehensive picture of you, your family and your business.

5. Give yourself some time before posting anything online.

Chapter 3
Violated by Your Own Name

I know who I am...don't I?

In 1967, North America was introduced to toll free 1-800 numbers. Some businesses were lucky enough to snag vanity phone numbers like 1-800-FLOWERS or 1-800-BUSINESS. For the next couple of decades, the scramble was on to own a toll free number that could be easily associated with a specific business. Scarcity propelled values higher and soon companies were bidding to purchase the toll free word numbers that gave them a competitive advantage. 1-800 numbers soon expanded to 888, 877 and 866 numbers. Nearly fifty years later, easily recognizable 800 vanity numbers are still used as both branding and direct response tools in business advertising and are proven to increase response rates. Vanity numbers like 1-800-FLOWERS and 1-800-PLUMBER are rare and quite valuable for company branding and advertising.

This discussion may seem insignificant in the evolution of commerce in America, but nothing could be further from the truth. The arrival of 1-800 numbers allowed for a redefinition of "real estate." It was no longer only important to be located in the right spot, it was also essential to be available—*easily available*—by telephone. Location was no longer just a brick-and-mortar building, it was a *virtual place*. A business could be located in a nondescript warehouse space but still attract customers nationwide if it had a great toll free number. This reality ushered in global customer service, 24-hour availability and lower costs created by second and third world labor.

Enter on the scene another smart guy.

In 1989, Sir Timothy John Berners-Lee, a British engineer and computer science professor at MIT, wrote a proposal for what would eventually become the World Wide Web. The convergence of toll free numbers and the correlating Uniform Resource Locator (URL), which is the "address" of a web page on the Internet, proved to be a virtual gold rush for every company, ad agency and marketer in North America. A company that was forecast for growth simply could not be without these two indispensable tools. Real estate had been redefined again. Phone numbers and website addresses that were virtually free in the beginning quickly took on values that exceeded what many companies were paying for offices to house their businesses. In 2006, it was reported that AT&T paid over $1.32 million to acquire the vanity number 1-800-YELLOWPAGES in combination with the sale of the domain name 1800yellowpages.com. The domain name 1-800-company.com transferred for $10 million in 2008.

This evolution has led to an explosion of companies that, armed with a website and a toll free phone number, establish global brands and enormous balance sheets without the need for any fancy office space! Business real estate is no longer limited to a physical, tangible brand or business, and this reality has spawned a global marketplace for website addresses. Domain auctions, bidding, drama, victory and defeat can now all be virtually experienced on sites such as buydomains.com (I wonder what they paid for *that* website?) and dozens of others all operating as virtual businesses.

While this short history lesson may help to frame the concept of owning your own virtual real estate, we have sidestepped an important dynamic that has shifted culture in ways that we do not yet fully understand. That dynamic is *you*. Simply put, in today's world you not only exist in a physical form, you exist in a virtual form. Because a website domain name (URL) is an address that is presented in alpha/ numeric characters, your name can be—and in all probability is—a website address. Assuming that you place value on your name, can you think of any real estate more valuable to possess than your URLs?

Your name has great value in the form of your reputation among peers, friends, associates and the community at large. We recognize this truth intuitively. In fact, your name is perhaps the most valuable thing you possess. Honor, integrity, trustworthiness and character are all wrapped up inside a few letters defined as your family name. As the saying goes, it takes decades to build a reputation but only a few moments to destroy it. This is what I will spend the balance of the book exploring.

When you are finished reading, you will have accumulated valuable information that empowers you to begin the process of repairing, reclaiming or defending your online identity. The starting point? There is only one thing that matters—your name. *You must own your name.* If you don't own it, then someone else can. And if someone else owns it, then you have no control over it, and if you can't control it then you can be violated online *without any ability to protect or defend yourself.*

Morgan Freeman learned this lesson the hard way. Yes, *that* Morgan Freeman. Freeman and other celebrities like Nicole Kidman, Sting and Julia Roberts did not own their online names—their *virtual selves.* Several years ago the *Shawshank Redemption* movie star learned that his name, MorganFreeman.com, was being used without his permission to make money. In 2005, Mr. Freeman won the rights to his domain name through a process involving a trademark filing and arbitrators for the World Intellectual Property Organization, an arm of the United Nations. Other celebrities have also successfully (and unsuccessfully) waged legal battles to obtain their already purchased domain names from cybersquatters.

A *cybersquatter* is an entity that has registered—in bad faith or with the intention to profit from—another person's domain name or trademark. Most of the time a cybersquatter registers the domain name with the idea of selling it to the actual name holder for a profit. In 1999, President Bill Clinton signed into law the Anti-Cybersquatting Consumer Protection Act (ACPA) that created a legal pathway for the owners of a trademark to file suit, collect damages and recover their personal domain name. ACPA allows the offended trademark owner to obtain injunctive relief and receive up to three times actual damages. The mark owner can also choose to collect anywhere from $1,000 to $100,000 instead of actual damages. For more information on the issues with which Sting, Jerry Falwell, Alanis Morissette, Celine Dion, Bruce Springsteen and Kevin Spacey have dealt, read the *Reports Committee For Freedom Of The Press*.[17]

If you're thinking, *Well, I could just file a lawsuit*, stop right there. It's not quite that easy. Several major steps must be taken before you can file a lawsuit based upon ACPA. First, trade marking your personal name is imperative. Second, you must be able to demonstrate that the registered domain name is "identical or confusingly similar" to your trademark. Third, you have to show the motivation of the offending individual. In other words, did they register the domain with bad intent?

Back in 2003, a mediation panel denied the late Rev. Jerry Falwell's bid to gain control of Internet domains bearing his name that posted criticism about him.[18] The Falwell.com website included an animated photo of Falwell inserting a foot in his mouth repeatedly. Dr. Falwell attempted to prove that a world-wide ministry had earned his name common law trademark status, but failed to meet his burden before the panel. After Falwell left this life and the Internet behind in 2007, the litigation ultimately prevailed (the site now points to Falwell's Thomas Road Baptist Church), but at what cost? The outcome of this case should serve as a wakeup call. You cannot dismiss lost time, lawyers' fees and court costs.

Evaluating all of the options may carry you to the conclusion that it is a whole lot easier—and much less expensive—to simply *own your name now*. While there may be legal precedence to help you acquire it after the fact, it will probably be costly, difficult and time consuming. If you don't own it, someone else can, and if someone else owns your name as a website then they control the content, and that includes any kind of content—political, religious and adult—*anything*. You can be compromised and violated in ways you cannot imagine.

Have you never considered this issue until right now? Are you ready to take action? Let me hold your hand and walk you through the process. Here's what you need to do:

- Open a browser window and go to www.godaddy.com.
- Type your name in the box that says *Start your domain search here* and click *GO*.
- Pray. Then pray again.

That final step is very important since you have absolutely no control over the availability of the domain version of your name. If you have lived a clean life, been kind to animals and never been arrested you may see the following: *Yourname.com is available!*

If, however, you see a message that says, *Yourname.com is already taken. View alternative results below or search again,* don't give up yet.

There is still hope! Attempt other iterations of your name. For instance, if your name is Michael Smith, try:

- MikeSmith.com
- Michael(middle initial)Smith.com
- Michael(complete middle name)Smith.com
- Dr(professional designation or title)MichaelSmith.com

You get the idea.

Continue until you have exhausted all possible combinations of your name as a dot-com URL. You will see that the second portion of the box allowing you to enter a domain name also provides a drop down menu. This menu, located on the right hand side of the box, provides additional potential options such as .net, .org, .info, .biz and so on. Think of these as the equivalent of toll free 888, 877, 866 telephone numbers. If available, they will suffice. Then, depending on your line of work, business and/or any current issues with online reputation, you may want to consider buying a few domain names that contain your name paired with a few "colorful" adjectives. After all, does owning just your .com or .org protect you from being violated by your own name? I'm afraid not.

How many different variations of your name exist? How many derogatory descriptions can you attach to your name? Going back to our example name "Michael Smith," let's say that Michael's middle initial is "James." Now we have Michael James Smith, Michael J Smith, Mike James Smith, and so on. This gives us the following potential domain names:

- MichaelJamesSmith.com
- MichaelJSmith.com
- MikeJamesSmith.com

- MikeJSmith.com
- *...and so forth*

Now let's get creative with this. Add to all the domain names above the word—*sucks*—e.g. MichaelJamesSmithSucks.com, MichaelJSmithSucks.com, MikeSmithSucks.com. For that matter, add any combination of colorful words to the domain name. Better yet, grab a piece of paper and add those colorful words to your spouse's name, your kid's name, and your company's name.

In December of 2010, *The Wall Street Journal* blog ran an article entitled "439 Ways to Hate Bank of America."[19] Author Shira Ovide related that those hating the bank, for one reason or another, now have "439 fewer ways to express their *Grinch-ness* towards the bank." It appears that Bank of America purchased and registered 439 Internet domain names with the potential to offend or be critical. Some of those domain names included the name of CEO Brian Moynihan. And the folks at Bank of America were creative with the possible word choices. Other companies, according to Ovide, have also made it a defensive strategy to purchase such domain names. This strategy may cost them a lot of money, but the expense is weighed against the ramifications of not following such measures.

Once you have searched your name and maybe a few colorful additions it will be time to complete your "insurance" purchase. GoDaddy.com provides a simple four-step process for purchasing a URL:

- Search your name (you just completed this)
- Register
- Customize
- Check out

For the purposes of taking the most direct path toward securing your online name, do the following: On the GoDaddy page, click *Add*, advance through the bulk pricing option box and click on *Continue* to registration. Depending on what version the GoDaddy site is running, you will be given the option to purchase all of the URL extensions for your name. If you choose not to do this, click *No Thanks* to continue.

The next step is *Domain Registration Information,* and this is a critical one. In all probability you will not already have an account with GoDaddy so you will need to populate the fields and set one up. Take time to read both the Registration Basics section and the Legal Policies.

Next, you will be taken to the *Customize* step. There is a dizzying menu of options, many of which you may not be familiar with.

Registration length is presented in yearly increments from one to five years; it's your call. You do not need a *Certified Domain* for the purpose of simply securing your URL. Again, for your immediate purposes ("insurance"), you do not need the *Deluxe* or *Protected* upgrades.

Scroll down to *Select Checkout Preference* and click *No thanks. I'm ready to checkout.*

In the checkout section you will again be presented with a number of options. You do not need most of the options suggested. **There is one exception**. Under the Quantity section you will see an option to *Add Private Registration*; check the box. Clicking on the blue *Why* link will provide a box that explains something very important. Here is what it says:

> *You should know that the information listed on your domain name has to be made publicly available per our Registrar's agreement with ICANN, the international governing body of domain names. Using false information will violate the registration agreement and lead to the termination of your domain registration.*
>
> *However, we do offer a solution to help protect your privacy. You can register your domain name with us using our private domain name registration services.*

*When you purchase our private domain registration services, the WHO-IS directory will list Domains by Proxy's name, postal address and phone number instead **of yours**. Although Domains by Proxy is the Registrant of your domain name registration, **you still retain the full benefits of domain registration**.*

That's right, you can purchase your URL, register it in your name, choose not to disclose publicly who owns the URL and still be in compliance with the law. In the interest of not being further violated (due to your personal contact information being provided to a global public), this is highly recommended.

Now, select your method of payment and continue. You will be asked to acknowledge the Universal Terms of Service for GoDaddy. Check all three boxes and continue with checkout. Complete the billing information and make sure that your email address is correct. Click *Place Your Order* and you will then be presented with your *Confirmation*. Print this out and keep it somewhere safe. I suggest putting it with other important documents such as your will and Power of Attorney.

If you have never before purchased a URL, congratulations! You now *own yourself*. I do have several additional thoughts on this subject before we move on. First, by methodically requesting the various configurations of your own name as provided above, you can see how it might add up to thirty URLs. But by taking advantage of the "bulk purchase" option presented as part of the purchase process it would only cost $100-$200 annually to own all of the versions of your name. In my humble opinion that is very inexpensive insurance.

Second, just because you now own these URLs does not mean that you have to "do" anything with them. Think of them as a plot of raw land that is now owned in the event that you want to build something there in the future. Finally, lead your family and friends through this process. Your spouse, your children and your business partners all need to own their online identities. When you give a baby gift, consider giving a URL. Securing a baby's name at birth is a gift that keeps on giving!

Throughout the ages, real estate has had value and solidified a person's standing in his or her community. In this "new" world, we now function in one unified digital community—whether we embrace this reality or attempt to ignore it. Real estate ownership remains the one irrefutable asset that continues to establish your personal value.

Five Things to Remember

1. You must own as much of your own real estate as financially possible.

2. Absent owning your name(s) as websites, you are exposed.

3. Legal recourse against cybersquatters is expensive and risky.

4. You need Private Registration on your URLs in order to protect your identity.

5. Spending money on an ounce of prevention is so much better than pursuing a cure.

(As you will see…)

Chapter 4
Violated with the First Click

A personal online experience is not as private as you think.

Yes, you are being tracked.

"It can't keep going up!"

Maria had been our client for about six weeks. She'd hired us after a co-worker's accusation about an inappropriate relationship with her manager had been replicated on more than a dozen online sites. Even her life partner was questioning what was going on.

Reputation Advocate deals with this type of slander all the time. We had successfully influenced the content found under her name so that her search returns were now honest, transparent and true. We explained that the project truly *had* accomplished her goal, but her panic was palpable. *Don't you see what the first thing that people see says about me?!!* An upcoming job review and potential management position hung in the balance and she couldn't be convinced that what *she* was looking at was not what *the world* was seeing when they searched her name.

We knew right away what the problem was.

Since retaining our firm, Maria had been searching her name and clicking on the complaint sites daily to see if anything new had been posted. But the more she reviewed the slander, the higher the complaint climbed in page rank. Maria had no way of knowing that her search results were being manipulated. She was seeing results all right, but Google was personalizing them *to her specific computer*. We sent her off to a library computer to calm her down.

For most people, using a computer means finding and using information on the Web. In a real sense, the beginning of any online experience requires three things—a computer, an Internet connection and a search engine. While there could be a whole book written about the different ways users are manipulated through search engines, we will look at just one—Google Personalized Search.

As of September 2011, Google received 67% of total search traffic and is, in fact, the first website to which most people turn. It is not uncommon for someone to ask, *Have you googled it?* Even aggressive moves by both Yahoo! and Bing have only allowed for modest gains in market share, with Yahoo! at 16% and Bing at 13%.

Utilizing these search engines and perhaps other smaller search platforms, users are able to search the vast expanse of the Internet for precise content. Type in a search for restaurants in your hometown and you will be presented with any number of links to reviews, maps and even online menus. While most people never question how these search results are determined, here's the reality: Even this basic function offers the potential for you to be manipulated unaware. While the basic Google page may seem straightforward enough, there can in fact be tens of thousands of calculations taking place across the Internet for each query you make. The results you see on your computer are probably unique to that specific machine. *That* was Maria's issue. By going to the library and typing in her name on the computer there, she was able to see her *true* ("universal") search results. Maria had never been told about *personalized* search results, but now she understood.

Every search submitted to Google will deliver 10 results per page, many times reaching on into near infinity. Search results are always tied to what is typed into the browser window—the search term and combinations of words or "keywords." Keywords are the terms that describe the person, product or service for which you are searching.

Let's say you were looking for a plumber. You might type in *plumbing repair*; the word *plumbing* and *repair* are keywords. Keywords and combinations of keywords deliver specific, targeted results. Every computer has a "fingerprint" of sorts. This unique ID identifies every computer in the world; it is called an *IP address* and is a unique number that identifies the computer and its location on the Internet. If you know the IP address of a computer you have very powerful information.

Blogger Chris Pirillo explains it this way: "Your IP address is what logs you into any of your email accounts; everything you do on the Internet is tracked. Searches, page views, clicks, ads you've been served— your Internet provider, your IP, the time of day—whatever possible demographic information can be retrieved. This isn't meant to make you paranoid, but you do need to be careful—in other words, be aware of the footprint you are leaving on the Internet. Unfortunately, creating a digital footprint is part of the deal you make when accessing the Internet. You ask for information and you get it—on the condition that the entity you've asked (and possibly others) will take some information for themselves."[20]

What this also means is that your search results will be unique to you. One of Google's search innovations was creating *instant search* and other *personalized search* capabilities that examine individual search habits and then use this information to alter, manipulate and modify the search results you see whenever you perform a query on a specific computer.

Your information is analyzed without your being aware of what is happening. Both Google and Bing use personalization features that operate under the rationalization of providing more relevant results. The search engine algorithms look at search history and remember which sites you usually click on. If you repeatedly click on negative postings, your search history is indicating that you have a high interest in those sites. And so, in attempting to be helpful, the search engine then raises these negative sites higher on the page for your easy viewing pleasure… *on that computer*. The Google website explains how personalized search works and how to disable it:

Search history and settings: Turning off search history personalization
Google sometimes customizes your search results based on your past search activity on Google. This customization includes searches you've done and results you've clicked. Since personalized search treats signed-in and signed-out users differently, the instructions for turning off search history personalization are a little different in each case.

Signed in searches
To disable history-based search customizations while signed in, you'll need to remove Web History from your Google Account. You can also choose to remove individual items. Note that removing this service deletes all your old searches from Web History.

Signed out searches
If you aren't signed in to a Google Account, your search experience will be customized based on past search information linked to a cookie on your browser. To disable these types of customizations, follow these steps:

1. *In the top right corner of the search results page, click the gear icon, then select **Web History**.*

2. *On the resulting page, click **Disable customizations based on search activity**. (Because this preference is stored in a cookie, it'll affect anyone else who uses the same browser and computer as you).*

Or, if you'd rather just delete the current cookie storing searches from your browser and start fresh, clear your browser's cookies.

Note: If you've disabled search customizations, you'll need to disable it again after clearing your browser cookies; clearing your Google cookie turns on history-based customizations.

Now that you realize that search results can be artificially manipulated, you may still be thinking that at least you can safely check email without being tracked. After all, email is the most basic function people look to the Internet to provide. No manipulation and it's safe, right?

Maybe not.

Even those that have been most resistant to technology have embraced email. My in-laws are eighty and spend several months each year living in a travel trailer. Their computer is a six-year-old hand-me-down and they don't have high-speed connectivity but they are plugged into the Web through email.

At the end of 2010, Wikipedia reported that there were over 193 million users of Google's Gmail. In February 2011, hundreds of thousands of those users lost all of their emails. *Poof!* More specifically, emails, labels, themes, folders and other personalized settings had been erased.

While Google was eventually able to restore the information over time, this incident speaks to the level of vulnerability to which we allow ourselves to be exposed. Even if you dismiss this as just a "glitch" in the system, Google has a larger and more ominous issue that has been consistently brought up for the past six years—privacy.

According to a MediaPost.com report, *Google has been hit with a second potential class-action lawsuit for allegedly violating people's privacy by serving contextual ads to users.* It states that, utilizing personal emails, individuals are targeted for ads relating to the content in their email![21]

The complaint, filed in 2011 by Texas resident Kelly Michaels, alleges that Google violates federal wiretap laws by *scanning and capturing the contents of every email sent and received through Google's Web-based email program.* If this sounds over-reaching to you, read how Google responded. They filed papers asking the court to dismiss Dunbar's lawsuit. Among other reasons, the search giant argued that the federal wiretap statute applies only to interceptions without the consent of one party. **Gmail users, the company argues, give Google permission to scan their emails when they sign up for the free service.** (I'm sure those users were aware of that.)

Privacy issues will always be of concern. The fact that the global giant acknowledges that they are in fact scanning email should, at the very least, give you pause. No, it is not slander and it is not blatant manipulation of the search results you request. *It is however an absolute violation of your privacy.*

On his website bruceclay.com, Bruce Clay discusses a judge in San Francisco that directed Google to hand over all the emails of a specific Gmail user, including deleted ones. The case before the court involved a credit counseling company that failed to use a customer's money to pay the creditors.

> *All documents concerning all Gmail accounts of the plaintiff ... for the period from more than a year, including but not limited to all e-mails and messages stored in all mailboxes, folders, in-boxes, sent items and deleted items, and all links to related Web pages contained in such e-mail messages.*[22]

We should not assume that we'll never find ourselves in a courtroom with our digital laundry on public display. Perhaps the surprise comes with the realization that the button branded as "delete," *doesn't.*

Manipulating search results, tracking your search queries and scanning and retaining all of your emails might have been considered basic civil liberties violations twenty years ago but these are the new realities of the digital frontier. Just remember that when you log in, the game begins.

It is a game that people have no chance of winning. It is a game that most people aren't even aware they are playing.

Five Things To Remember

1. What you see for search results may be different from anyone else's.

2. You must deliberately log out of Google Personalized search.

3. Your entire online experience is analyzed, evaluated and tracked.

4. Search engines retain your email for a period of time—even if you delete it.

5. Your digital footprint can walk right over you.

Chapter 5
Violated by Family, Friends
and Employees

There's a lot of truth that shouldn't be passed around.
Gossip doesn't have to be false to be evil.

Shortly after Christmas we received a call from an agitated young woman. She got right to the point, saying, *I understand that you help people with Internet stuff—I need help!*

Usually, when we hear these cries for help they come from someone embarrassed by an online posting that was pointed out by a well-meaning friend. This call, however, was different. It seems that the family Christmas dinner hadn't gone so well. Excusing herself from the table, this woman had pulled out her Android smart phone and by the time everyone else was done with the pumpkin pie she had posted some very unkind things about the rest of her family.

The call I received came a few days later when she came to her senses. She had searched her father's name, then her mother's. It was all there. Her panic on the phone represented remorse, but it was too late. The sites on which she posted will never remove her comments—*never.*

She hung up, devastated that her quick temper had created misinformation that will follow her family forever.

No one can hurt us as deeply as those closest to us. A combination of history, vulnerability and shared memories commingle with feelings of unforgiveness, shame and pride, and they create a dynamic like no other. Sibling turmoil is recorded in an early biblical story about Cain and Abel, and endless family dramas have played out on the stages of history. Juicy stories are splashed across the front pages of both printed and digital newsmagazines everyday. Our own country references folklore from the West Virginia Hatfields and McCoys and there are many tales of brother fighting brother during the War Between the States. History clearly demonstrates that ill will can be held between family and friends for generations. When we carry this truth into our digital age, the only thing that's different is that the weapon of choice goes from a knife to a digital laser.

From sibling rivalries to animosity between former spouses, many family members are moving their disputes and disagreements to a world stage—the Internet. We have read about and personally witnessed many ugly scenarios. Parents recently deceased, an estate working its way through dissolution and jealousy over issues from the past are shamelessly discussed on the planet's largest social sites. Issues dating back to adolescence, undocumented loans made by parents and not repaid—what are brothers to do? Apparently, duke it out on a cyber-stage for all to see.

Repercussions from online disputes can take many forms. In April of 2010, Arkansas resident Denise New was sued by her sixteen-year-old son for harassment and slander after she allegedly made some unwelcome comments on his Facebook page. Charges of harassment against Denise were filed and a *No Contact Order* was issued after her son convinced the local prosecutor that his mother had posted slander about him on Facebook. He also alleged she hacked his account and changed his password.

Needless to say, Ms. New was more than a little embarrassed. She said she was simply monitoring his page because she was concerned. Her son's friend had informed her that her son had posted about speeding with other teens in the car. *I read things on his Facebook about how he had gone to Hot Springs one night and was driving 95 m.p.h. home because he was upset with a girl and it was his friend that called me and told me about all this that prompted me to even actually start really going through his Facebook to see what was going on.*

Whether attacked by your child, your brother, your mother or your friend, an attack is always an attack. And when it is placed online, issues that might be better resolved in private become fodder for the world. Wounds such as these may not technically fall into the category of *slander* but the damage is just as real. Just listen to George and Sarah's sad tale.

George and Sarah were married for fifteen years and over the years their extended families became close and grew to care for one another well. But when broken vows delivered divorce papers to this family's door, the embarrassment and shame led to questions about who was to blame, a natural outcome of this very painful process.

We have spoken several times in this book about the dynamics created on Facebook. The Facebook *Wall* is an area on each user's profile page that allows "friends" to post messages or photos. A user's Wall is visible to everyone with the approval to see his or her full profile, and those Wall posts may also show up in a friend's News Feed. Many users use their friends' Walls for leaving short, temporal notes.

So how many people can see your Facebook Wall? According to Facebook statistics from May 2011, the average member has 130 friends. Since many people have their sharing permissions set to "friends of friends," (Facebook's current default setting), it's possible that you have been sharing not just with your own friends, but also all those who are friends of your friends. That would mean sharing information with potentially 16,900 people! While George and Sarah likely had fewer virtual spectators, a little basic math allows us to see the breadth of exposure that can be created *without even realizing it.*

One reality of the Facebook wall is that those whom you have deemed *friends* have the ability to both read and post on your wall comments. As the news began to spread, notes of comfort appeared on George and Sarah's Facebook walls. At first they were sweet and gentle. Family members avoided publicly choosing sides and attempted to be supportive of both. But bubbling just underneath the outward civility were feelings of betrayal and a sense that someone needed to be defended and protected. Aunt Elsie's Facebook post on Tuesday at 10:34^{PM} put into words what everyone else was thinking, and suddenly the rumblings took on a life of their own.

This was the first time that George and Sarah actually realized how exposed they were online. George and Sarah recalled Christmas 2010 when they had discovered the Facebook application *Family Tree.* [The application is offered by Familybuilder (www.familybuilder.com), a New York City based software company that builds family/genealogy applications for social networks. The Familybuilder flagship product, Family Tree, is the leading genealogy application on Facebook today.] Building a family tree was appealing to them so it was only natural to sit, notebook on lap, and spend several evenings hunting for family on the largest social network in the world. Most of their family members, having the opportunity to join the family tree and *friend* those joined by marriage and heritage, also welcomed the opportunity to draw closer together through technology.

And thus, the disintegration of their marriage was further complicated by the connectedness that one hundred and eighty seven relatives had established online. As comments were posted, everyone in the tree saw them. *Everyone*. Before long, names, indiscretions, locations, financial information and long repressed memories were displayed for all to see. Parents were shocked, siblings were angry and the children were hurt and confused. The real time delivery of this sniping so escalated over a single weekend that George and Sarah became the most measured and civil family members living in their virtual tree.

On a Tuesday morning, the call we received was a teleconference that had been set up to pose a single question, *what could be done?* Since Facebook users have the ability to control, accept and delete friends from their wall, George and Sarah could access their own Facebook accounts and remove the relatives they were no longer connected with, but they had no ability to disconnect the relatives from one another. With their divorce decree final, assets divided and recovery groups on Thursday night, George and Sarah were attempting to move on with life, but not so it would seem for their relatives.

In fact, an interesting dynamic often found online is that the willingness to keep a feud going is much more pronounced. Deliberate violations are not the only pain that can be delivered through the Internet. Love and a marriage gone badly can create widespread collateral damage. Irreconcilable differences are never just about two people parting ways. Parents, children, distant relatives and friends choosing sides can mean that even the most thick-skinned gets hurt. Using the Internet spreads the infection deeper and wider—and much more quickly.

But this scenario is not restricted to family issues and it doesn't need a Facebook app like Family Tree to create the same dynamic. Dating relationships with mutual friends create similar drama. The lessons this story offers focuses on a simple realization; once people are digitally connected you lose control of the dialogue.

Two sisters lived through a similar nightmare.

Close in age, Susan and Sandy grew up in a large Minnesota city with parochial values, solid academics and wonderful role models of parents loving each other well. Their family was close and they walked through their teens as friends. Susan, the younger sister, found academic success challenging but whatever she lacked in grades was made up for in her social interests. By the third year of college she was engaged and her fiancé was quickly integrated into family vacations and holidays.

Susan and her husband graduated from college and began life modestly with a few possessions. A baby arrived on the heels of their first anniversary. Sandy was there for everything and was truly happy for her sister. Their parents gifted the young couple the twenty percent down payment necessary to avoid private mortgage insurance and they moved to the suburbs.

Sandy's life progressed quite differently. Academic excellence, finding identity in achievement and few opportunities for romance delivered Sandy to the stage of a respected university where she graduated with a medical degree and the designation of Radiologist. Great money, predictable hours and a settled life provided security and safety for the single sister. But then life took an unexpected turn— Alzheimer's. *Times two.*

Following an eight-year process of gradual memory loss and ever-expanding care requirements, Susan, Sandy and their mother were almost relieved at the passing of their father and husband. But neither daughter could have seen or imagined the illness and near passing of their mother shortly afterwards; it hit too fast. The need for her care fell to the sisters. Susan had a family to care for and so Sandy stepped in to look after their mother. Her medical background was helpful and being single, she could spend a good amount of time with her mom. When their mother died, she left an estate to be settled and property to be distributed. And sisters who had been close since birth began the painful process that every family must eventually address.

Sandy was named executor of the estate. Both sisters attended the official reading of the will and realized that when it was written some twenty-seven years prior, there was no attempt by the parents to address the details the girls would face. This meant that they would have to do what they had done their whole lives, work things through together.

Sadly, that did not happen. Sandy's sharp memory regarding the house down payment and Susan's eye on several pieces of furniture created a split—a vindictive one. Sandy had full access to the house since she had cared for her mother and so it was only natural that she began to move items out. Learning of this, Susan launched into a full-blown online rant. I could go on and on—like Sandy did when she called me but I won't. As the disagreement over possessions continued, the conversation turned increasingly personal. Finally, Susan demanded that items be delivered to her, or she would come with her husband and get them. She didn't have to wait long.

Sandy delivered the furniture, a rug and boxes of childhood memories to Susan's front yard—in the pouring rain. Smug and satisfied, Sandy knew that by the time Susan got home they would be ruined. Before she left, she pulled out her phone and snapped pictures for posterity. Later in the day as a steady rain continued, Sandy sent an email to Susan with a photo attachment. And this is where the story turns. Sandy called our office ready to not just tell the story but to justify her actions, and in conclusion she explained the email.

Many times when people call us, a long portion of the conversation is the caller telling us what we should think, believe, accept or affirm about them. Sometimes I think we should charge by the minute and provide online counseling! In this case, when Sandy was done talking, we simply suggested that she contact a local law firm that could present her situation in court when the time came. Was this online slander? *No.* Was it damage done online? In this case, *yes.* Was it stupid?

Absolutely, We hear about estate settlement disputes every month. One adult child recounted the lack of care for a deceased parent as they faded away and how a sibling's financial deception regarding monthly expenses spilled digitally on to the Internet. One interesting dynamic seldom considered is the court's ability to use such information, as long as the individual posting has conclusively identified himself. Boasting and pride does indeed come before a legal fall, especially in a family.

So what can be done about these types of online family disputes and situations? The short and direct answer is that civility and dialogue provide the most comprehensive solutions, because at the point of conflict the Internet can be used with precision to destroy families, and most people don't have the presence of mind to think things through.

As with families, close relationships between friends, employees, or neighbors can also be a blessing or a curse.

Sixteen thousand dollars a year for a prep school education was steep, but Ethan's parents made the sacrifice. Ethan was exceptionally bright and his parents wanted him to have the opportunities they never had. His senior year was a stand out. The college level courses came easy for Ethan and with good grades came the offers for academic scholarships. Ethan's character and consistent involvement in civic and charitable activities made him the perfect candidate for an Ivy League school.

Ethan's good friend David had also done well in high school and expected to be offered the gift of a higher education. Ethan's opportunity knocked but David's did not. While David was outwardly happy for his friend, the jealousy began eating him up. A visit to a couple of social sites, the use of Ethan's "identity" and a few compromising pictures from a party presented Ethan in a much different light than the colleges believed him to be. As a result, both young men now have student loans and attend state universities part time as they work their way through school.

Another story is that of Frances, who owns a lovely condominium in Virginia, right outside of Washington D.C. When her husband passed away several years ago, he left Frances with the means for a comfortable retirement. The complex she selected seemed well suited for her. It was a senior center with small yards and pets. However, Frances soon realized that her neighbor was not a person she would ever choose to live next to and they simply did not get along.

There was always something brewing, and by the fall of 2010 things bubbled to the surface. While she was away visiting grandchildren, the neighbor raked all of her leaves into Frances's yard. When she returned home, Frances called the property manager and wrote an angry letter to the homeowners association; her neighbor found out. Over the next few weeks, a number of online local real estate blogs received very caustic comments about the property management company and in particular, the complex that Frances lived in. Each posting was simply signed *Frances*.

Frances was completely unaware until a knock on the front door delivered a court summons notifying her of a lawsuit being brought by the property management company and the homeowners association. Frances currently has her condo on the market and is looking for a new place to settle.

Then there is the sad tale of a local dry cleaner.

This independently owned small business had been hit by the economic downturn and fewer men were paying $2 to launder a shirt. The owners were facing a grim reality; they must lay off their office manager. While the employee seemed to understand that there was no other option, the owners had no idea she had sworn revenge. Postings began appearing on several complaint sites that alleged misappropriated funds, payroll taxes not paid and discrimination and sexual harassment. They included the names of the husband, wife and both of their children.

The dry cleaner operated by factoring their receivables through a bank line of credit. The bank had recently changed its underwriting guidelines, and when credit lines came up for renewal even long-standing customers were re-evaluated. Part of the routine due diligence included online search results and the very first posting trumpeted the former office manager's unsubstantiated claims. Because the banker, focused on remaining employed, was unwilling to take any form of risk that might negatively impact her career, the line of credit was not renewed. The business owners were forced to close their dry cleaning establishment—the terminated employee, however, continued to receive unemployment.

Each of these stories is real. The outcomes have the same thing in common—innocent lives damaged by someone who was close to the victim. The sad reality is that there are many more angry, malicious and vindictive people living around us than we want to admit. While it's not so hard to believe this in the abstract, it *is* nearly impossible to accept the fact that we interact with them everyday without realizing where they live in their minds.

I often say that stories like this *have* to be true because no one could easily make them up. The ease of posting content on the Internet has allowed character flaws like envy, greed and jealousy just one more conduit for expression. Remember that harmful information can come from the most unexpected sources. Until you are able to see the reality of this statement you may never realize who your attackers are.

Business owners often have a strong suspicion about who has attacked them. They recognize details of a complaint but have no recourse against the anonymous posting. In fact, horrible things posted on social sites nearly always come from someone close, even a friend. Most of this negative content will never be removed.

Without moralizing, let me offer an observation: conflict resolution usually takes time. Most of us have been advised to *take a deep breath, calm down* and *give it a little bit of time.* These well-worn sayings capture one simple truth. Sometimes in the middle of a conflict or disagreement the thing needed most is *time.* Time yields perspective, and with a different perspective misunderstandings and conflicts often resolve themselves. When given an immediate, anonymous "voice," many people who are otherwise kind and rational strike out on impulse without ever considering the ramifications. The absence of time coupled with the immediate gratification of unloading can explode like gasoline and a spark.

Many times it's the person closest to you that does the greatest damage. He or she takes information about your life and uses it against you. You may or may not recognize the source of these online disclosures. Awareness is your number one tool for defense because unaware, you may continue to see the person as a trusted confidant and keep on disclosing your pain and your plans.

The good news is that you *can* repair and reclaim your online persona over time. But as you begin the process we urge you to be cautious with whom you share your online plans and goals. There is nothing sadder than someone who takes measured action to repair damage, only to find that the attacker is aware of every move they are making.

A question remains, however: *What can really be done?* The answer depends on where the negative content is found. If slander is found on a blog, you may be able to identify who is hosting the site and contact them directly. Negative comments are also posted on the "comment" sections of many websites. Again, if you can identify who controls the site then a firm request or a certified Take Down Demand[23] may deliver results. This type of approach may also allow your attacker to evaluate how committed they are to hurting you. Legal action is time consuming and expensive for both parties.

A warning, however—contacting your attacker may agitate the situation and direct additional efforts against you. We caution people to seriously evaluate the probability of a positive vs. negative outcome before making a call or sending a letter.

If specific personal information such as a social security number or business FEIN, banking information or other confidential information is disclosed in a post, this may be a violation of the Terms and Conditions of the site operator or Internet Service Provider (ISP). Read the fine print on the site. There are usually instructions for contesting content. Just note that absent a specific violation, even Terms and Conditions will provide little relief.

Five Things to Remember

1. If you are slandered online, there's a good chance it's been done by someone you know.

2. Impulse is the enemy of a rational decision.

3. Online conflict takes on a life of its own.

4. Awareness is your number one defensive tool.

5. Offensive content does not necessarily violate the Terms and Conditions of most sites.

Chapter 6
Violated by the Little Things

Catch for us the foxes, the little foxes that ruin the vineyards.
Song of Solomon 2:15

Brian, a successful entrepreneur in Northern California, had built a well-diversified business that provided nicely for his family. Like many self-made success stories, Brian was respected as a savvy professional and often asked to serve on various boards and committees or speak on behalf of civic and philanthropic organizations. Brian's values and beliefs motivated him to support causes that mirrored his outlook on life and culture. Brian's religious affiliation led him to take conservative positions about lifestyle issues and conduct. His perspectives on civic matters positioned him in opposition to certain groups and politicians, and Brian's confidence provided a certain bravado that drove him toward higher visibility and more than a little bit of controversy.

Each year offered numerous invitations to political fundraisers, and Brian seldom missed them. Rubbing elbows with local influencers and meeting local, regional and national political figures could only help his business, he thought. But bidding on a local government contract would prove to be far more challenging than he had ever imagined, thanks to public policy regarding contributions to not-for-profit organizations, political action committees, or directly to politicians.

An informal conversation over a pleasant lunch meeting brought up the topic of Brian's political contribution history—information he assumed was private. He learned that websites like *campaignmoney.com* and *fundrace.com* document campaign contributions by individual, party and cause. He was told that Sunlight Foundation uses cutting-edge technology and ideas to make government transparent and accountable. On the foundation's website he read the following:

> *The Sunlight Foundation is a non-profit, nonpartisan organization that uses the power of the Internet to catalyze greater government openness and transparency, and provides new tools and resources for media and citizens, alike. We are committed to improving access to government information by making it available online, indeed redefining "public" information as meaning "online," and by creating new tools and websites to enable individuals and communities to better access that information and put it to use.*[24]

Sunlight's position sounded reasonable to Brian until he realized that it applied to his political contributions. He went online to the Federal Election Commission website fec.gov to see what might be done to veil his giving and was shocked to read that his contributions were not just a matter of public record but were also posted online! In searching his name he found that the third posting on page one was fundrace.huffingtonpost.com. Results delivered by clicking the link blindsided him. Not only were his contributions to specific politicians disclosed but much, much more. His eyes caught two things, including a disclosure that:

FundRace is updated according to the reporting schedule set by the FEC. Public contribution data is geocoded using public U.S. Census Bureau Dynamic maps are powered by Google Maps.

And there it was... a map to his house! Yes, the site had tied his contribution to Google Maps and offered his information to anyone bothering to look. Feeling exposed, Brian was shocked by this violation of privacy. Campaignmoney.com actually offered a button with the caption "Download all contribution records for this person from 1999 to present." *Twelve years!* Clicking on a PDF file delivered schedule A of the Federal Election Commission filing complete with his home address, the contribution amount and the benefactor of his gift.

The reality that those reviewing his bids on government contracts could easily define his political allegiances was very disturbing. Having this information used against him as a weapon had never been a consideration, and Brian's high profile made him a visible target.

Then Brian found another listing near the middle of page one, and this one proved to be the most damning: A controversial state proposal relating to gay marriage had compelled the state's largest newspaper to write an article about *Proposition 8: Who Gave in the Gay Marriage Battle?* Listed in the article was a $100,000 contribution against gay marriage linked to Brian and his company.

Brian's political contributions, coupled with information about him on a religious website, clearly defined him as a political and social conservative and an individual opposed to a number of popular community initiatives. Government contracts suddenly became much more challenging!

Now meet Natalie. She called our office to get some basic information about online reputation management. Natalie was vague and not willing to offer much information early in the conversation. When people are hesitant, we pro-actively offer information about our company and point them towards our Better Business Bureau relationship. People often need familiar touch points to get more comfortable before they reveal details.

When she finally opened up, we learned that Natalie's situation was heart breaking. Trapped in a marriage a decade prior, she was the victim of domestic violence. The beatings continued until she finally sought help and had a restraining order placed against him. Then life began anew and the nightmares began to fade away.

Remarried, she was now the mother of twin seven-year-old boys, had secured a good job and moved on. But one Tuesday after lunch she was called to her company's human resources department for an unscheduled meeting. The discussion came out of nowhere. Vague questions asking if help was needed for a "situation at home" made no sense. Totally baffled, Natalie asked what the Human Resources director was talking about. The woman handed her a piece of paper along with words of comfort: *It's safe, you can tell me.*

There were the police records and restraining order, front and center on page one of Natalie's search results. Absent the records of the subsequent divorce, a second marriage and children, a conclusion had been made—a *wrong* conclusion. Natalie's explanation satisfied her employer, but Natalie was panicked at a more basic level. Her husband and children knew little about the early history of her life. In fact, her husband knew nothing of the spousal abuse. She had meant to tell him but it was all so unpleasant and the need seemed to pass when life was good again. All it would take for this issue to threaten her husband's trust was a single search of her name from him, a friend or her children when they grew older. The information was not slanderous—it was totally and completely accurate. But Natalie felt exposed, vulnerable and violated.

Though different in the details, Brian and Natalie were dealing with the same basic reality—they were being violated by what I have called the "little things." Brian's views and political contributions and Natalie's tragic past were exposed for all to see on the Internet. It's often easier to head off the large *known* violations online, because there is time to prepare. But as with much of life, it's the little stuff sneaking up from the shadows that can hurt the most. This chapter is but one arrow pointing toward the hundreds of "little things" found online that can damage a reputation.

So, how did all of these potential violations come to be? As previously mentioned, the Electronic Freedom of Information Act Amendments of 1996 states that *agencies must provide electronic reading rooms for citizens to use, providing access to records.*

Before the Internet, public records were essentially private because of their obscurity; they sat gathering dust in courthouse files in city, county, state and federal offices. But since the late 1990s, courts have posted records online to manage cases more efficiently and provide easier access. While convenient, many online records now provide information about what has always been considered private matters. Political contributions, adoption files and tax liens are not the only public information that can be easily found online. There is the potential to find information about your glory days as a high school athlete or charitable contributions and birth records that are decades old. Clearly, any business owner who has given politically or had any minor legal scrape can be at risk.

Today's crime victims, jurors and witnesses fear that they can be easily identified and located. Others worry about identity theft. Former inmates want their pasts hidden, not publicized. Divorcing couples grumble that their neighbors now know their business. All of this is very challenging when viewing Public Record sites such as http://www.publicrecords.onlinesearches.com, a free directory of public records links. The site positions itself in this way: *PublicRecords.OnlineSearches. com provides thousands of links to free public record searches in every state and county in the United States.*

There is no easy way for content found on public record sites to be altered or removed. Information found on these sites ranges from property, marriage, litigation and civil and criminal actions. ZabaSearch.com is a free people search and public information search engine. Again, this information includes residential phone numbers and addresses and is aggregated from public sources. Many times there is a list of the homes and phone numbers that you have used historically.

Can you begin to see how this information could be used for secondary purposes? A homeowner considering hiring a contractor for a home improvement project, a prospective patient checking out a particular medical professional, or any consumer curious about the services of a small business may very well make a decision based upon the "little things" they discover online. If you consider highly paid professionals immune from these issues, think again. Medical professionals have more than seven rating sites including vital.com, ratemd.com, healthgrades.com and zocdoc.com. Most of these listings are inaccurate because the initial general information has simply been gathered from state licensing boards. Many times these listings are never even claimed by the medical professionals and updated. Some of these sites are so outdated that they actually list deceased doctors and the insurance plans that these dead doctors currently accept!

So, how damaging are these sites to the medical community? Visiting the site of medicaljustice.com provides some interesting reading. The site offers this information:

The Problem of Physician Internet Libel and Web Defamation
As a physician, one of your most valuable assets is your reputation. Anonymous web postings by disgruntled patients can threaten your good name and practice. Most medical practices are built through word of mouth. It only takes one negative Internet posting to impact your livelihood.

The company expands on its explanation of the challenges facing medical professionals today.

On rating sites, patients, or people posing as patients—such as disgruntled employees, ex-spouses, or competitors can damage a hard-earned reputation. And a doctor has no recourse. As an arcane nuance of cyberlaw, the web sites are immune from any accountability. (Section 230 of the Communication Decency Act).[25] Many sites have generally taken the position they will not monitor or police any content.

Issues relating to a patient's experience, disappointment with the care received or a less-than-attentive office staff can end up following a doctor's career forever. In fact, all vocations—the butcher, the baker and the candlestick maker—can be the target of impulsive and immature statements, and none of them have to be true to inflict damage upon the victim.

Blending and combining several online sources provides a comprehensive profile of who you are, where you live and a number of activities you are connected to—information that used to be much more challenging to obtain. By searching your home address on zillow.com anyone can determine the square footage of your home, its value, your property taxes and surrounding home values. A click to Googlemap.com will allow a virtual voyeur to actually look at your home, see your landscaping, your driveway and your neighbor's homes. This level of exposure drives people to indeed feel violated online and offline.

A final concern surrounds feedback and rating sites like Citysearch, Yellowbot, insiderpages.com, Google and Yahoo! local, and Angieslist. All of these general rating sites offer a double-edged sword for small business. While accumulating positive ratings is always a plus, negative ratings and comments can never be removed. A "thumbs up" or five-star rating this month can translate to thumbs down and a one star rating weeks later. The bottom line on these types of sites is that you may not be able to edit the information offered by others, even if it's inaccurate. Some sites offer the opportunity to provide a rebuttal, however any rebuttal may be perceived as being defensive and actually reinforce the perspective of the low rating.

So what do you do—live in denial of a reality being delivered to anyone who cares to look? Perhaps not. However, you must engage. You have to know if your past is being read in the present. Half the battle for many is that they are completely unaware of past events being placed online, *until it's too late.*

Step two is simple. Get help. Because even if you ask nicely, websites displaying public records do not have to remove the information. The only way to deal with historical information may be to push it farther into the past—to suppress it.

Five Things to Remember

1. Political contributions, affiliations and political parties are a matter of public record.

2. Legal documents forgotten or never acknowledged publicly may surface at any time.

3. Public information gathered from multiple sources can radically expose you.

4. Living in denial and attempting to wish it away does nothing.

5. Even if content cannot be removed, it can be influenced.

Chapter 7
Violated by Comments

He who knows how to flatter has the abililty to slander as well.

I was in the fifth grade. At that time my body was growing in an asymmetrical manner and balance was an issue. At five foot five, 118 pounds and wearing a size 11 shoe, I didn't have to worry about falling over, but walking was a different story. I was also the oldest son of a man who lettered in three sports (albeit from a *very* little school). He was a football, basketball, baseball man. From the description of my physical stature you can probably guess that my first foray into athletics was baseball. Little League in Iowa was big—real big. I made the team, although looking back on it now probably everyone did. But to me it was a big deal.

Fast forward to the season opener. I was in right field and had never played in a real game before. There was a high pop fly and my failure to reach the ball before it hit the ground was further aggravated by a throw to home plate that missed its target by a good twenty feet.

Like all kids in sports of any type, I could hear my father's voice as though no one else was making a sound. And boy, did he have an opinion. The person sitting next to my dad, a guy I did not even know, learned from the most influential voice in my life that I was *just clumsy, not very athletic.* It was my first failed attempt at being a jock. That is all it took. I never went to another practice, and was then labeled a *quitter.*

I tell this story for a reason. My father said something that day without thinking. He had no clue that his comment would live on in my memory almost fifty years later. If he knew how long it would live he might have kept quiet. Throwaway comments can be powerful, even damaging. Kids learn this early, first because we are the targets and also because we learn to use them against other people. Webster's defines comment as *a criticism, remark, observation or interpretation, often by implication or suggestion.*

Let's look at the concept of online comments and where they can be made.

- Social sites
- Consumer sites
- Rating sites
- Blogs and Forums

In the context of the Internet, Webster's definition really nails it. While there are some sites such as complimentworld.com, most comments fall on the negative side of the equation. I want to take a look at each one of the forms mentioned above.

But before we go any further, let me say that by the time you read this book, *THIS INFORMATION WILL BE DATED!* Why? Because social media is moving at such speed that there is no way to put into print the most current and accurate information on these sites. For now, let's continue with some basics.

Social Site Comments

Again, let's start with the mother of all sites, Facebook. We'll limit our discussion to the comment capabilities of the site. If you already use Facebook, you'll understand the concept of writing comments on another person's wall. For the seven of you that don't have a Facebook page—yet—here is a brief explanation.

Facebook allows you to invite "friends" to connect with you. These friends become part of your private network of approved friends and you can then engage in a written dialogue with them by posting comments on each other's *Wall* (profile page). You can make a comment to someone or someone makes a comment to you.

Right away you can see there is the issue of privacy. If I take a step backwards to Facebook 101 class, here is the basic structure and design of this comment function. Once you are a *friend* of someone, you can see their friends and then request that their friends accept you as a *friend*. So let's say that your business has not taken time to set up an official Facebook Fan Page and instead has a traditional (personal) Facebook page. You use it to market to your existing customer base. Your customers become your friends and once they accept you then they can see all of your other *friends*. In other words, customers have the potential to connect with, or *friend*, other customers, employees can friend customers and visa versa. Once they are connected, they can see comments placed on each other's wall.

Now let's add a couple of dynamics. Imagine an employee dialogues with a client and a client comments about service and that is posted on your company's Wall. It's easy to see where this might lead. In fact, this aspect of social media has the potential for great good and greater harm. An internal network of friends is open to every "friend" and their comments. Now take that power and place it on dozens of websites. Think about it. There are real concerns for privacy. Fortunately, Facebook recently released its latest version and provides tools to address this issue.

Utilizing Facebook allows you to share almost every aspect of your life through photos, links, videos, virtual gifts, your interests and random musings in the form of status updates. By "being social" and "participating in the conversation," Facebook friends post a great deal more information about their lives than they might offer in a person-to-person conversation, and it all seems so natural. What serves users well is Facebook's many features that allow individuals to choose the features they do, or do not, want to use. By setting up *friend lists* and adjusting privacy settings, it is possible to create access to different areas of information for each group of friends in one's life, both personally and professionally. Facebook friend lists can be used for a variety of purposes. However the single most significant benefit for the average small business user is that it is now possible to organize lists of *friends* and then adjust Profile Privacy Settings. You can establish *Potential Customers, Work Relationships,* or *Employees* and then adjust privacy settings to control each list's level of access.

Whether you are an individual or a business owner with a general Facebook account, how much you're inclined to disclose on Facebook depends upon a number of factors and can change based on what your latest marketing efforts involve, who has recently joined the network, or what your overall goals and use of the site are. But a basic breakdown looks like this: your public listing should be carefully planned. Adjust the settings of your company's public profile. Allow individuals who aren't connected to your Facebook account to view general company information, in case a potential employee, customer, networking contact or former associate is looking for you. To do this, make the company profile available to "My Networks and Friends" and your search visibility to "Everyone." You should also make sure that the "Public Search Listing" box is checked so your company's profile can be indexed.

Now decide what you *don't* want non-friends to see and change these settings, allowing "Only Friends" to see that information. This also sets up the all-access version of your profile for your friends. "Safe" stuff typically includes Basic Info, sales and employment information (depending on how much detail you provide), product and territory information and contact and location information. That means no photos, no videos, and no wall. Applications with a more professional focus, like your blog or Linkedin profile, are also okay.

With all that said, at the time of this writing ten privacy and consumer groups have filed complaints with the U.S. Federal Trade Commission alleging that Facebook Inc.'s privacy-policy changes violate federal law. This saga will continue as social media channels like Facebook attempt to expand and redefine what our virtual future will look like.

So, the first issue was privacy. Our second concern is liability. Once a comment is posted on someone's wall or any social site for that matter, it can't easily be removed. While this is true of nearly all sites that provide the ability to comment, there may be a false sense of security about postings made in a "closed" network. Company issues are further complicated by the fact that one or more employees may be able to place content on a business site. Unlike your internal computer server or network, there is only basic security available. A login and password are the only tools necessary for an individual to set up an account. An individual posting content or comments on the company Facebook site can create unintended results that expose both individuals and companies. This is best explained by looking at two recent stories in the media, both Facebook-related.

Back in December 2009, President Obama made a speech about the war in Afghanistan. Arlington, Tennessee mayor Russell Wiseman was upset because he believed that the speech was deliberately timed to block the network-scheduled *Peanuts Christmas* special. Wiseman made some statements on his Facebook page. Although only people on Wiseman's friends list had access to his comments, there were 1,600 of them. One of his Facebook friends did a little "cut, paste and send," and the next thing he knew, the good mayor's comments were loose on the Internet.

An editor with Memphis, Tennessee's newspaper, *The Commercial Appeal,* read his comments and felt they were newsworthy. This paper provides an online version where online news aggregators can identify items of interest and post the content on sites viewed by a much larger audience. By December, things had grown to a decidedly different scale. What was originally meant for his friends was now news to the world. There on the front page of the *Drudge Report* (drudgereport.com, perhaps the largest single web news portal in the world) was an article exposing the mayor's thoughts to the world. That day, the *Drudge Report* had over 25 million visits. While there was no liability on the part of the Memphis paper, the Arlington mayor was now a point of relentless scorn, and future elections will no doubt be tough for Mr. Wiseman. What can we learn from Mr. Wiseman's mistake?

- Understand your friend lists
- Control contact information
- Avoid embarrassing wall posts

Now let's dig into the liability issues. Here is a true story from my hometown that says it all. A suit was filed in Davidson County, Tennessee for libel, slander and intentional interference with business relationships.

The owners of popular Music Row watering hole, The Tin Roof, filed suit against Brian Manookian. They say he defamed their business with a Facebook Wall posting suggesting that their restaurant had been the scene of a serious crime.

The defense for Manookian alleges *he obtained the information contained in the Wall post from public police records.* The outcome is actually a secondary issue for my purposes. Acknowledging that litigation can occur at any point in the life of a business, we all strive to avoid such expense. Apply this litigation to an employee/client/vendor situation, and my point has been made.

Business comment and rating sites

My friends ate at this place and got food poisoning! The manager's girl friend, Sheena, is horrible. It's like she thinks she owns the place.

The owner of a small restaurant had no idea where this comment and the accompanying single star rating came from. He also could not help but notice that his fiancée, Shawna had her name misspelled. Would you say this comment came from a customer or a terminated employee?

Feedback from clients, customers, neighbors and vendors can always be helpful in business. Sites like Citysearch.com, Yelp.com, MerchantCircle.com, angieslist.com, yellowbot.com, Google Places and Yahoolocal.com all offer a voice to friends, employees, customers—and competitors. Predictably, there is a shadow side to these sites as well. Each of these sites and many others allow for posting comments and the ability to rate service and performance. Because these postings can be made by fictitious people, comments can be untrue, false and harmful to the business being mentioned. Most of these sites also provide the ability to "rate" a business. Some use stars, smiley faces, some thumbs up or down and others a numeric score.

In all cases, if your company has only a single comment with a rating that is poor, your business will appear to have a very low score when presented in a search. Unfortunately, when a thumbs-down or frowning face is seen, many people simply go on to the next business indexed for the search term.

Imagine a competitor, disgruntled employee or customer having a bad day. They can take advantage of these scoring functions and suddenly you have issues. The majority of calls we receive regarding this type of problem have to do with manipulated comments and ratings. *Do not underestimate the power of these simple rating sites.* In general, people do not take time to evaluate the credibility of a comment or rating. All they might notice is a frowning face, and that can equate to lost business.

There *are* solutions. The very best thing to be done, right now as you read, is to go online and see what is currently posted for your business. You may be surprised or even horrified. However, *do not overreact* and start posting rebuttals. First, review the current information about your company. You may find that even the basic contact information is incorrect. Many sites have content that has been pulled from general online public records and is inaccurate. Your business may not have "claimed" the listing. Look for a link that says, *Is This Your Business?* or, *Suggest a Correction.* Then you can correct and complete the information.

Some of these sites offer a "premium" service that allows you a great deal more control over content and images if you subscribe. Costs range from $5 monthly and up and several are connected with phone directories. Correct all of your information, load your logo art and make sure that the contact information is accurate. Claiming your business identity, reviewing the existing information, uploading art and pictures and monitoring the comments posted will help you quickly evaluate the value of the site and credibility of the offered comments and ratings.

What you want most is authentic feedback. The easiest way to acquire that type of input is to *ask for it.* You have clients, vendors and other relationships that appreciate you, your employees and your company. Ask them to log on and leave honest comments and ratings. Do not, however, have everyone do it over a short period of time, or it will appear that someone has artificially manipulated the additions and they will be discredited. Take a methodical, measured approach and lay out a plan. Have two or three people per week for six to eight weeks add information. Any negative postings can be diluted and pushed down, since most of these sites provide the most recent comments and ratings first.

Finally, visit your rating sites regularly, or delegate this task to a support person. Every Monday morning have someone quickly look to make sure all is well. If something has occurred that is not favorable, execute your plan once again. Don't over react and *stay vigilant.*

Blogs and Forums

There are some very basic things you need to know about blog and forum comments.

First, they come in millions of sizes, shapes and colors—literally. Virtually any company, individual, group or organization can set up a basic blog in about five minutes. Some are beautiful, tasteful and complex. Others are bare bones and might rage against anything from the evils of herbs in our diet to tribal practices in New Guinea.

Second, blogs can damage your reputation as severely as any type of online post seen by the world. One reason for this is that they can be very specific and target you or your company. Just search the now infamous term *Dell Hell.* If someone is disgruntled at you, your employees or your company, you stand the possibility of being targeted.

Third, almost all blogs offer the ability to provide comments. As we have already discussed, *comments are never just comments.* There are three flavors of blog commenting when a blog is set up: (a) comments are allowed and can be posted without review or edit, (b) comments can be offered but are reviewed and then accepted or declined, and (c) no ability is provided to make comments so, in essence, the blog is not a dialogue but a monologue.

Fourth, you can create, write, moderate, edit and post a company blog—and you should. Many times corporate blogs are linked to a company website and offer the ability to write about current trends, issues and topics of interest. Readers can make comments and suggestions. You have the ability to review and edit this content before it is posted. This deliberate "censorship" will allow you to filter out derogatory, negative and inappropriate content that other readers might find offensive.

Fifth, when you are attacked on a blog, insert yourself into the conversation. This doesn't necessitate getting into an argument in front of the whole virtual world. The path of intelligent and civil discourse can occur and if that happens, you need to be in the mix. If civility is not acknowledged then stay silent. There is no winning scenario when virtual war breaks out.

By going to either Wordpress.com or Blogger.com you will be able to access everything you need to set up a blog, build a site from existing templates and get your content easily placed. This is simple to do and provides you with a virtual voice. Never underestimate the power of the written word. For a growing relevant business, this tool is not optional.

Five Things to Remember

1. Anyone can create a website.

2. Freedom of speech rules supreme.

3. Comments are never just comments.

4. You need to establish and participate in your own blog.

5. You need to stay involved in the conversation.

Chapter 8
Violated Through Conviction

You may experience something very painful
when you stand up for what you believe to be right.

Although the harsh winters of Minnesota were more than Ben had bargained for when he relocated to St. Paul in the early '80s, the city had been good to him. Starting with little capital, Ben's commercial electric business had grown almost every year. The building boom of the nineties had allowed his business to grow without debt in a solid manner. The company had over 300 employees throughout the metro area and had expanded into both commercial and residential services. Now in his late fifties, Ben had been able to transition management into the hands of solid operators and the business provided him the kind of comfort for which most of us hope.

Lunch with the assistant editor of *The Star Tribune* convinced Ben to take a stab at writing by submitting comments to the editorial section of the Minneapolis newspaper. After all, Ben was looking for a transition from the mundane. While not compensated, being recognized as a writer could be beneficial since *The Star Tribune* was the largest published newspaper in the state with a significant influence in the city, across

Minnesota and even into parts of Wisconsin, Iowa, South Dakota and North Dakota.

Ben found that within a short period of time he had defined his "voice" as a writer and was receiving positive feedback most of the time. After a bit of soul searching, he accepted a management buyout and stepped away from the everyday grind of commerce. The sale of his company garnered newspaper and television interviews, raising his visibility even further and he was recruited to various causes. Ben felt most comfortable among those of the conservative political persuasion and responded kindly to the various invitations. Rotary and Kiwanis meetings filled his lunch schedule and he fell into the rhythm of afternoon writing from an office at home. Ben had no idea how writing one simple editorial would change his life forever.

Holding to parochial values in the area of marriage and family, Ben believed that people around him—particularly those in the Methodist church where he'd been a member for thirty years—shared these common values. It was a natural extension then, for his worldview to extend to the keyboard and the writing of which he had grown so fond. The heading for this editorial piece was *Adam and Eve, or Adam and Steve?*—a morality piece with a catchy title that allowed Ben to express his perspective regarding what he saw as a fundamental shift in society's acceptance of alternative lifestyles.

The next day, his editor's phone lit up and by eight-thirty that morning it became obvious that a major nerve had been hit. The paper offered the opportunity for an editorial response and the spokesperson for a local activist organization jumped at the chance. The online version of the paper, startribune.com, carried both editorials and attempted a fair and balanced debate.

As it turned out, some members of the Silver Sneakers, the seniors group at Ben's church, had children that lived a lifestyle that—while not openly celebrated—had been integrated into the families of some of his closest friends. He was shocked to find that several who had attended his church for decades did not share his perspective and that members of his own Rotary club had also dealt personally with this issue.

After some serious soul searching, Ben realized that he had hurt people through his written opinions and he took the opportunity to apologize whenever he could. Ben was sure that over some short period of time things could be corrected and he promised himself that he would take a more measured approach in future editorials. But a series of events led several local activist groups to seize the opportunity to bring their oppression to the media's attention. Ben was now the poster boy for all that was wrong about the "far right" that could not accept individuals different from themselves.

A fifty-person picketing rally brought the broadcast trucks to his front yard. Ben's simple answers to direct questions provided just enough sound bites to satisfy requests and Ben retreated to his office and called the newspaper. The editors of the paper had a quick meeting and determined that it was in the best interests of the paper to suspend Ben's editorial voice. The newspaper published its decision the following day. Way beyond stunned, Ben was not capable of processing what had happened.

The activists, smelling blood, stepped up their efforts and took their message to the broadest and cheapest media tool available—the Internet. They started by linking Ben's article on the newspaper website to their own site. This allowed sympathetic people from around the country to read Ben's piece and comment on it. An email blast to a national database stimulated a national response and the email boxes of every editor at the Star Tribune filled quickly. Wanting to evidence the storm that Ben had created, the paper forwarded every angry email to Ben's email account. Within two days several thousand emails clogged his inbox.

A call from the church stopped Ben dead in his tracks. The church secretary provided enough credibility to assure Ben that the call was not a prank. *The news was impossible.* Ben turned on his computer. Typing in his first and last name delivered the confirmation. It was no joke. The first ten search results for his name were all tied to gay websites. Each site had other links and the whole of the content was shocking. The pictures had obviously been manipulated but no one would consider that fact if they casually glanced at them. Then there was his altered editorial along with a vicious narrative.

This could not be happening to him.

As he clicked the media tab on one of the websites he was taken to an interviews section with three links, all attributed to him. How had they done it? While the TV interview was not attributed to any station, there it was, the one he had done in his front yard just a few days ago. But it was not *his* interview. The words had been restructured to make statements that he would never say, but there he was saying them! Outright slander, posted by people with "names" that reflected large body parts—no one real, nobody he knew, all part of the sham.

Again, a simple cut and paste of the link into an email blast delivered Ben's distorted interview and pictures, and this time the names of the editors of many major media outlets had been included along with Ben's phone number and email address. It was all too much. Ben knew nobody he could call. The shame was overwhelming because all he could envision were his friends and people in the community gathered around their computers. He kept clicking on the sites, hoping the content would change; it did not. Finally his wife unplugged the computer and Ben collapsed under the weight of it all.

Ben had no alternative; he packed up his SUV and headed to the fishing cottage for a few days of solitude. A few days turned into a few weeks and Ben slipped deeper into depression. His friends in Silver

Sneakers had scheduled a three-day weekend to Lake of the Woods to admire the fall foliage; he did not go. Rotary and Kiwanis continued their weekly meetings without Ben. Hymns were sung and sermons preached in church on Sunday, but Ben benefited from none of it. The worst part was, the longer he was gone the more it implied that he was actually guilty of what had become a national media exposé about hate and prejudice. His comfortable retirement had turned into a most uncomfortable hell.

Ben stayed up late, night after night, trying to figure out how to get his side of the story out. But the newspapers had no interest—it wasn't sensational enough. Multiple unreturned phone calls were evidence that after five weeks radio and TV considered it yesterday's news. No one wanted to hear him. Ben's children called him daily, attempting to speak words of comfort but without much success. They were in as much disbelief as their father and searched for an answer to rebut this great injustice perpetrated on an honorable man. Ben's youngest son Philip was in his last year of an advanced degree at Miami University, and he invited his father down to spend a few days in the sun—to get away from the cold, both literally and figuratively. Ben arrived in a flannel shirt and corduroys, suitcase in hand. Maybe this trip would at least provide some much needed rest.

Like most of his peers, Ben's son Philip was a tech-savvy grad student who had taken both on-site and virtual classes, who accessed his class notes via the Internet and tweeted constantly. Such daily participation in social media was so common within his circle of friends that he never considered it might seem foreign to his father. But lacking knowledge of the Internet beyond email and a couple of news sites, Ben's exposure to social media was very limited. He began exploring some of the sites suggested by his son and found a broad forum for thought that seemed unrestricted, yet intelligent. Ben continued to read and began to understand how the sites providing his slanderous images and articles were created and why they were so predominant in his search results. He asked for help from Philip, and together they defined a strategy. Ben had finally found a media source that would allow him to defend himself. His name, coupled with vulgar words and salacious comments, was right at the top of his search results. He learned that once postings are ranked high on the first page of search results they are very challenging to influence, but he began to realize that they *could* be influenced.

Ben's re-education had begun.

His son explained how search engines worked, that his name was a *Keyword* or *Search Term* and that his name could be integrated into a blog. Philip told Ben that anyone could have one or more blogs. By using his keyword/name effectively, Ben's blogs would begin to appear when his name was searched. Content could be posted instantly and was only limited by the time he had to write and post his blogs and the number of people that chose to follow his writing. Philip told him that the more people that read his blogs, the more relevance his blogs would have. Ben was *hooked*.

Ben immediately went to work putting his new skill set into practice. First, he streamed a podcast from Southern New Hampshire University and then found workshops on "New Media for Activists and Campaigns" and "Facebook and Twitter for Political Communications" posted by Newt Gingrich. He was very taken by the concept of these websites and in particular the blogs. Going to Wordpress.com and Blogger.com allowed him to set up accounts and the sites walked him through the steps necessary to establish his online voice. Within days, Ben had a dozen social sites all providing solid accurate information about his life. He had found a way to begin to fight back!

Ben's story ends as a work in progress. He still retreats to his office each afternoon to write. There are a few less lunches outside the home; friends are funny that way. He is back with the Silver Sneakers, although a bit less vocal. The assistant editor of *The Star Tribune* follows Ben's blogs and provides comments, although never using his real name. Ben has indeed found a group of like-minded people around the country and they are avid readers of Ben's cautious yet thoughtful articles. Ben has a Twitter account, is followed on Facebook, has reconnected with friends from high school and found a voice on TownHall.com. Ben's first blogged editorial was titled *What Happened?*, and it explored in retrospect what had transpired over the last eight months of his life.

Ben got a painful education in social media, the global reach of the Internet and the ominous ability for anyone to write anything anonymously at anytime without accountability. His second article was on the provisions for freedom of speech found in our Constitution. Ben's perspective was that *our founding fathers could have never foreseen the global ramifications that such freedom has. Unlimited access to technology, spontaneous broadcast, no civil decorum and the Constitution have combined to unleash a very real weapon of mass destruction on an unprepared population.*

So what can we take away from this short story? *Reality.* In business there is an age-old axiom—never bring up politics or religion. More friends, neighbors, business relationships and family gatherings have been damaged over these two subjects than any others. Ben is living proof. Conduct ranging from shouting matches to the silent treatment, children not being allowed to play with the kids of "those hippie liberals," the defacement of holiday symbols representing a family's faith—we have all heard about this kind of craziness. Letters to the editor and petitions have allowed citizens to loudly express their political and religious opinions since the founding of our nation, and these two topics demonstrate the deep passion people have for their convictions.

Over the last twenty years or so, our country has seen the rise of national newspaper ads and television commercials funded by ordinary citizens who have organized to pay for such media efforts. (Many of us can remember Ross Perot running for President or major oil companies defending their conduct.) We have seen national newspapers run full-page ads that champion conservative and liberal ideals. These forms of public advertising have been limited to those who have either had deep pockets, Political Action Committees or not for profit-tax exempt status. While that has provided a broad national platform from which major entities can be heard, what about us commoners?

Ben's story answers that very question. With access to the Internet and its ever-broadening influence, *We the People* have been given a voice. There are no cost barriers, for public libraries provide Internet access to all. Online, there are no conduct parameters. There are rarely editorial boundaries that frame a debate and no across-the-board requirement to respect another person while disagreeing with his or her views on an issue. I believe that defining those boundaries in the heat of debate requires a certain discipline that has been, for the most part, set aside. We as a society are the poorer for it, but getting the genie back in the bottle will probably never happen.

But as a blogger, you can use the tool, respect your readers and encourage those sharing differing perspectives to speak to the issues and stay away from the insults. You have the ability to act as both moderator and editor. It's your blog.

Five things to remember

1. Prominence and respect in your community can be fleeting when confronted by media.

2. When you are violated online, even those in your corner may not know how to come to your aid.

3. Those that understand technology will always have the upper hand.

4. If you don't know how to protect yourself online, ask for help.

5. Ben's reality could end up being anyone's reality.

Chapter 9
Violated by the Immediate

Impulse is the enemy of the rational mind.

Scandal-scarred Rep. Anthony Weiner resigned June 16, 2011. His downfall came not from a public policy issue or controversial proposed legislation. It came because of a salacious photograph intended to be sent as a private text (*sext*) that was instead launched as "send all." Weiner was quickly sucked into the media firestorm that erupted over additional lewd pictures and messages that he sent to several women on Twitter and Facebook over a three-year period. At first, the seven-term Democrat claimed that his social media accounts had been hacked, but finally admitted that it was simply very poor judgment on his part.

Earlier in the year, Katie Couric had fired off a tweet saying that Egyptian President Hosni Mubarak had resigned. The date was February, 2011, and the incorrect bit of news was quickly re-reported by a *Daily News* staff writer. Couric, then the CBS News anchor, informed her 140,000 Twitter followers that Egyptian President Hosni Mubarak had stepped down after 30 years. *As many of you have already heard, Mubarak has resigned,* Couric tweeted, before backing off the report. But one hundred and forty thousand people received the incorrect information within seconds. And many of those 140,000 forwarded (re-tweeted) this news to their followers so that within minutes the world was provided misinformation.

If this were an isolated story there would be little use for further discussion. But many times a harmless "tweet" morphs into literally a billion snippets of spontaneous thought that is released into a galaxy of readers with no ability to remove, retrieve or rehabilitate any of it. That is very sobering.

Spontaneous tweeting in a weak moment can expose poor judgment at the same time as an unsuspecting victim is attacked. Recently, themoneytimes.com reported a story that could haunt any corporate executive. It involved actor/director Kevin Smith, who was asked to deboard a Southwest Airlines flight upon which he had booked a seat. Drawing upon his savvy in the finer arts of tweeting, Kevin's outrage exited through his figures as he launched a tirade:

> [Tweet:] I flew out in one seat, but right after issuing me a standby ticket, Oakland Southwest attendant Suzanne (wouldn't give last name) told me Captain Leysath deemed me a "safety risk".
> [Tweet:] Again: I'm way fat... But I'm not THERE just yet. But if I am, why wait till my bag is up, and I'm seated WITH ARM RESTS DOWN."

Though the actor was accommodated on another flight from Oakland to Burbank and even given $100 travel voucher for the trouble he had to face, it did not mollify him. He continued tweeting:

> [Tweet:] I'm on another one of your planes, safely seated & buckled-in again, waiting to be dragged off in front of the normies.
> [Tweet:] "This is my last Southwest flight. Hopefully by choice."

He landed in Burbank and he tweeted again. The whole incident received a lot of public attention. Many of Smith's fans took to Twitter and various blogs criticizing Southwest Airlines' customer service.

Realizing the seriousness of the situation, the airline apologized through Twitter and its blog and addressed the concerns raised by many.

> *First and foremost, to Mr. Smith: we would like to echo our Tweets and again offer our heartfelt apologies to you. We are sincerely sorry for your travel experience on Southwest Airlines.*

Despite the apology issued by the airline, Smith continued to vent his ire via Twitter. He condemned the airline for lying and tweeted he is not a regular two seat buyer as mentioned by Southwest.

> *[Tweet:] Writing that buttresses their lie: 2 Fat 2 Fly.*

He also added that he is not too fat to occupy a seat and the armrests went down so he could even buckle the belt. Another of his postings read:

> *[Tweet:] Dear Other Airlines, I'm in the market for a flight east this Thurs. Which one of you likes fat people?*

Where has this kind of power come from? With thumbs flying on an iPhone, fact and fiction blend together like a frozen margarita and deliver a more potent kick then any happy hour. Twitter has changed how business must respond.

Sports Illustrated recently ran a story pointing to the consequences of impulsive texting.[26] The May 16, 2011 edition of the magazine reported that Pittsburgh Steelers running back Rashard Mendenhall challenged America's reaction to Osama bin Laden's demise in a series of postings on Twitter. His tweet read: *What kind of person celebrates death? It's amazing how people can HATE a man they have never even heard speak,* and was followed up by Mendenhall wondering whether planes really could have taken down the twin towers on 9/11. The 23-year-old had signed a four-year extension to endorse Champion sports apparel through 2015, but the company announced after reading the tweets that, while it respected Mendenhall's right to express his opinions, it no longer believed he could "appropriately represent" the brand. While we will always embrace free speech, this incident clearly points to the price that can be paid due to impulse.

I remember getting my first Motorola satellite Skypager in the 1980s. At the time I traveled a lot, and mobile communication was still married largely to pay phones. After landing in an airport, I'd check my pager to see if there were calls, run for a phone and check my messages. (When I tell my kids this story, their eyes roll back in disbelief.)

I would write down the message and number, dial the phone, punch in a long distance credit card number and act as professional as I could, given the environment I was in. But back then, this was the acceptable way of doing business. Skypager was the first national paging platform I had access to and it revolutionized my ability to do business on the road. It was state of the art technology. Considering that physicians in the New York City area introduced the first practical pager in 1950, it's hard to believe that it took nearly forty years to go from city paging to national paging.

Now, let's jump ahead to 2006 and the launch of Twitter as a social networking and microblogging service. The text messages that are passed back and forth on this site are referred to as *tweets.* Text messages are individual posts of up to 140 characters displayed on a user's profile page. No more running to a phone to listen to a message, no more waiting for a return call. No more checking email; that is soooo "yesterday"! Twitter alone facilitates a billion tweets a day and that represents a lot of unfiltered thought.

Tweets are publicly visible by default, although senders can restrict message delivery to just their followers. Users may subscribe to other users' tweets—this is known as *following* and subscribers are known as *followers*.

All users can send and receive *tweets* via the Twitter website using compatible external applications (for smart phones, iPads, etc.) or by Short Message Service (SMS). So now that I've given you the basics, let's take a look at concerns.

While Twitter is all the buzz today, many business people are still hard pressed to find its practical everyday applications. We read about tweeting largely in the context of what twenty-somethings do, however while you may not be personally affected by Twitter, its relevance is all around you. Twitter creates great influence for individuals, companies—even politicians. The most powerful aspect of Twitter is that a message goes *instantly* to the sender's entire list of followers. From there, the message can be "re-tweeted" to all of the people on each one of the followers' lists.

Dialogue plays out online in real time. Persons receiving the message have followers who can read the original message when it is re-tweeted. Then, the people who are following the followers of the followers can see the message. And after that... get the picture? It's confusing, I know. But let me provide a couple of practical examples that display the power of Twitter.

Obviously, when business owners read about incidents like Southwest Airlines and Mendenhall experienced, they flinch. The spontaneous ability to communicate whatever is happening real time has changed the rules. If we understand that Twitter can impact business, the relevance to our lives becomes more applicable.

In fact, Twitter is so influential that the most powerful man in the world tweets. In a 2011 tweet to his 6.4 million followers, President Obama asked, *Can you host a State of the Union watch party next Tuesday?* The tweet went on to say, *On Tuesday, January 25th, President Obama will deliver his second State of the Union address. To help get the word out about the President's vision for the next year, OFA volunteers will be holding State of the Union watch parties and strategy sessions across the country—and if we're going to have enough events in enough places, we'll need your help.*

For those still skittish, another tweet followed: *Don't worry—no experience hosting an event is necessary, and we'll provide all the materials and guidance you'll need to be successful. Simply use the form to the right to get started.*

Business and politics can be influenced by 140 characters, and that is impressive. If that opens your eyes, hang on. What if 140 characters broadcast to the world real-time could actually impact the world? Let's remind ourselves of what prompted Ms. Couric's well-intentioned but incorrect tweet—a revolution! Many credited the overthrow of Egypt's ruling party with Twitter's instant ability to communicate and mobilize the masses.

Imagine that you, your family or an employee text or tweet a simple opinion on any subject. One of your followers agrees and re-tweets it to their 150 followers. Out of the 150, one follower thinks that the opinion is based in bigotry. They re-tweet your original opinion to their 200 followers with a little addition: *definition of bigot.* From there those 200 followers re-tweet the new message commenting about you to…*how many people?* Now do you see how a simple message can have weighty consequences?

For many people, relief may come as they walk through this process in their mind and conclude that (unlike email) tweets disappear and fade with time. That might be true were it not for a public commitment that Twitter, Inc recently made.

Perhaps you missed the April 14, 2010 headline in the *New York Times* that read *Library of Congress Will Save Tweets.* That's right. *Everything* you have tweeted. Everything that has been tweeted is now being archived in the Library of Congress. (Ironically, the Library of

Congress announced the acquisition of the Twitter archive via their Twitter account.) All Twitter text messages dating back to early 2006 are now in federal files. Could our government access these tweets looking for language, terms, buzz words and patterns that could be used to *further violate* Americans online? I'll let you draw your own conclusions.

So now that we have demonstrated that Twitter is a tool that can be utilized to do damage online, let's look at some basic approaches to protection. This will not be an exhaustive "how to" but rather a basic beginning to protecting yourself on Twitter or other online communities that you participate in.

To begin with, if you don't already have a Twitter account, you will need to set up a profile. There are a couple of account settings I would like to suggest. First of all, you should decide if you want to give people the power to find you by searching for your email address. This decision can be determined by whether or not you have more than one email account, i.e. one for business, one for personal use and perhaps a third one for online social sites.

Second, you have the ability to provide your geographical location as you tweet. Twitter does retain your locations, but you can turn this function on or off at any time and the default setting is off. That's good. While there might be exceptions to this rule, we believe that it is generally not in your best interest to activate this feature. This Twitter function is now tied into Google and may actually deliver a map pinpointing your physical location. Think about it—is it *really* necessary that people know exactly where you are?

Under Tweet Media you will read, *By default, you'll only see images and videos shared by people you're following,* Again, for the average business professional there are not many advantages to changing this setting.

While you may have found these pointers helpful so far, they pale in comparison to the final option, *privacy.*

Protect My Tweets is the box that addresses many concerns. Basically, this feature allows you to accept or reject people that are interested in following you on Twitter. Businesses that establish professional Twitter sites may allow everyone to follow them since they are using the platform for promotional purposes. Twitter can interface with LinkedIn and identify your professional business relationships that are using Twitter and you can request connections to them. Conversely, individuals may only be interested in tweeting to a select group. Keeping the ability to select and reject those following, constrict the photos available and not allow your exact location to be determined are all safeguards to consider when using Twitter.

Twitter continues to adapt their services and after reading this book, I encourage you to go to Twitter.com and review the most recent updates to the privacy settings.

A caution regarding being violated by Twitter: Twitter doesn't censor information. Anyone you're following or receiving updates from can tweet essentially anything, including rogue links, ads and malware. Although these aren't included in the tweets themselves, links to other websites are common in the Twitter world and the majority of the time they should be avoided unless you know the person well. Unless someone is spamming you with large quantities of unwanted content, Twitter security policies are loose enough that people will be allowed to continue tweeting, regardless of whether they're offending or harming someone indirectly.

The final caution might go without saying, but I want to remind you once again that followers can tweet nasty posts concerning you, your family and your business. Twitter was never intended to act as censor and so again, anyone can tweet anything at any time and anyone following you will be able to read messages. Reflect for just a moment on the stories shared at the beginning of this chapter. Can you imagine yourself in the middle of a Twitter chat that turns sour?

Five Things to Remember:

1. Being attacked on Twitter can come with no warning.

2. You have the power to determine who will be allowed to view your tweets.

3. Be deliberate in choosing your Profile settings.

4. Make sure your message is something you won't regret.

5. Twitter was never intended to be a censor.

Chapter 10
Violated on Complaint Sites

Even doubtful accusations leave a stain behind them.
—Thomas Fuller 1608-1661

I will never forget the first time I realized how frightening it would feel to be stalked. The year was 1987, and I had just seen a disturbing film called *Fatal Attraction.* Just like that movie, our next story began somewhat innocuously—harmless flattery that evolved into something terrifying. Like the old saying goes, "Hell hath no fury...."

A distinguished professional, Dr. Wagner established a dental practice about thirty years ago in a large Midwestern city. A quality education coupled with integrity delivered him accreditation, admission to the American Dental Association, and membership in the American Academy of Cosmetic Dentistry. He built a good, solid practice and was enjoying the fruits of three-plus decades in his profession.

Enter the woman.

In this case, the interest was one-way and she really did need dental work. Then, her visits became more frequent and with them came tighter clothes, heavy perfume and eye contact that made it a challenge to look at only teeth. What she *didn't* know was that the dentist's wife and daughter both worked in the practice and were spectators to the whole parade. Maintaining a professional relationship, however, the doctor continued to provide the dental services that she requested and scheduled.

Dr. Wagner isn't exactly sure how or when she discovered the family ties, but one thing is certain—the woman felt that she had been made the fool. Usually when this happens most people quietly fade into the background, but not this time. Aggressive visits to the dental office, loud outbursts and even removal from the reception area by the city's finest did not deter her. Scorn turned to rage, and her rage soon demanded that a price must be paid by the good doctor.

The woman began by filing an official complaint about the services that Dr. Wagner had provided. But after a peer review by the ADA, no fault was found and her legal course of action collapsed. Her resolve to pursue the doctor did not, however. Then she found the Internet. And what could not be done in person or through legal action was accomplished in the solitude of her home whenever she felt so moved. And moved she was.

While the doctor had a simple website for his practice, for the most part he had left the Internet alone. Email, a little news, or an occasional search for a restaurant defined his experience on the Web. Like so many people slandered on the Internet, someone else—in this case a well-meaning patient—discovered the attack.

As Dr. Wagner entered his name in the search box on his Web browser, he was not prepared for what he saw. He'd never had terms like *fraud, scam, thief, liar, cheat* and *rip off* associated with him or his professional practice but there they were, for all the world to see.

His reaction was quite normal. *He panicked!* Truth is, until you are attacked, you have no idea how it will impact your emotions. It's really common to react with outrage. Most people react with great indignation and want to do nothing less than sue—*somebody!*

Because many complaint sites allow for rebuttal, most victims immediately start typing a defense. Such a reaction comes from such a place of rage that often the resulting postings are not even spell-checked. Such was the case with Dr. Wagner. A long, point-and-counterpoint rebuttal provided him satisfaction that *something* had been done. But now a trap was set and the real power of online slander could exact its revenge.

What most people don't realize is that there is actually an unwritten list of absolutes regarding complaint sites. Dr. Wagner was about to learn all ten of them, the hard way.

- *Rule #1: Don't process emotions through your keyboard.*
- *Rule #2: Never place a rebuttal on a complaint site…ever!*
- *Rule #3: Your added rebuttal on a complaint site may cause the negative content to rank even higher on Google, Bing and Yahoo!*

Once Dr. Wagner hit "send" there was no turning back. And while in his mind the rebuttal was eloquent and well written, most people would never take the time to read it. Unfortunately, the rebuttal allowed the complaint site to automatically create a second complaint sub-post, causing it to rank higher and become twice as visible in Google, Bing and Yahoo!.

For any search, there are currently ten results presented on any given page. At this point only twenty percent of the first page search results for Dr. Wagner's name had been impacted, but the woman had only begun. She learned the power of *Title* and *Meta tags*, the "headlines" for each post. By placing Dr. Wagner's name in the Title tag multiple times, her attack on him began ranking higher. The doctor was actually known by several names; Dr. Wagner, Dr. John Wagner, Dr. John J. Wagner and Dr. John J. Wagner DDS. Imagine her satisfaction as she created complaints for all of his identities. Sitting in the comfort of her home she picked apart his professional credibility and personal character, one posting at a time.

Over the next several weeks, Dr. Wagner watched the complaints continue to move higher on his first page search results. They seemed to¹ multiply before his very eyes. Websites he'd never heard about had detailed, slanderous comments about him. He hunched over his computer night after night, hoping to find an end to this nightmare, but soon realized that he was no Internet street fighter. Now Dr. Wagner was learning rule number four and five.

- *Rule #4: Negative content may be duplicated from one complaint site to another and you will have no control over this process.*
- *Rule #5: Things move very quickly over the Internet.*

There was no sudden decline in his business, no high drama—just a subtle bleeding away of what was once a steady stream of new patients. In fact, there is seldom a way to empirically define the amount of lost revenue to a business as the result of half-truths, lies or strategically placed slander. No one ever knows how many people read digital poison and pass along the newfound "knowledge" to others. Enter rule six and seven:

- *Rule #6: You will never know who has seen your information online.*
- *Rule #7: People rarely ask you if what they read is true.*

At this point, Dr. Wagner was so desperate to stem the tidal wave of garbage that he visited the office of an attorney, a friend of one of his children. The attorney listened empathetically and let the doctor vent about how wrong, how unfair and illegal it was…*it must be illegal, right?* It was then that the doctor learned the final three absolutes regarding complaint sites:

- **Rule #8:** *Slander is often posted anonymously and therefore it is usually impossible to identify an attacker.*
- **Rule #9:** *A website hosting derogatory content accepts no liability.*
- **Rule #10:** *The U.S. Constitution and federal law actually protects Internet service providers.*

Short of identified threats against the government, a victim's full social security number or the posting of child pornography, complaint websites are allowed to display nearly anything with complete immunity, since Internet content is protected by the Constitution upholding our freedom of speech. Complicating things further, the servers hosting these sites might not even be located in the United States. So, even if a victim can identify the source, get a take-down order issued by a court and have it enforced, by the time the process has any meaningful impact the damage is done.

Outrage, rebuttals, litigation and the hope of federal protection through law could not help Dr. Wagner's situation. He had come to the end of his rope. Patients and friends had read the postings and his revenue had been impacted. He had lost seventeen pounds and many nights of sleep. His anxiety level had not been this high since he received his draft notice for Vietnam. Where could he go and what could he do? Where would *you* go and what would *you* do?

Complaint Web Sites

It used to be that when a customer had a complaint about a product or service the dispute was presented to a creditable third party such as the Better Business Bureau or Consumer Affairs and a resolution was reached. This is simply not the case anymore. Hiding under a cloak of anonymity and empowered by a worldwide audience, complainers have carried their tirades into cyberspace.

Complaint sites typically collect stories of supposed bad customer service or faulty products. While most of these sites posture themselves as performing a valuable service for consumers or employees who have opinions, the true intent is thinly veiled. Hundreds of Internet complaint sites have become the weapon of choice for frustrated customers, disgruntled employees, competitors, political activists—anyone with an axe to grind. It's a way for individuals to air complaints cheaply, globally and many times effectively. While the vast majority of complaint sites fall into the category of consumer complaints, for this chapter we'll briefly examine two kinds of complaint sites: targeted websites and general complaint sites.

Targeted Web Sites

Commuters arriving in San Francisco using the Bay Bridge were confronted with placard signs reading: *Had any problems at Starbucks Coffee? You're not alone. www.starbucked.com.* A former customer had taken his anti-Starbucks campaign to the world and the Web, developing a targeted website site with a not-so-subtle domain name that bore a striking resemblance to the corporate name.

Companies face a challenging battle when attempting to take down this type of content. When the "complaint" site is engaged in commercial activity, Federal trademark infringement, dilution and trade libel laws may protect a targeted company against disparaging use of corporate names and trademarks and confusing domain names. Targeted complaint sites that appear on third party servers are generally subject to a web hosting agreement that specifically prohibits trademark infringements and offensive materials and language.

When receiving legitimate complaints of possible infringement and libel, hosting companies will generally remove such pages. However, when the purpose of the disparagement is solely customer opinion, perspective, complaints or parody, these laws provide far less protection. The list of these sites is growing daily and a few specific widely publicized examples in addition to Starbucked.com, are listed below:

Chasebanksucks.com

The Right Relationship Means Nothing! The Worst Bank in the Universe! This popular site features an animated picture of a man repeatedly relieving himself on the slogan *Chase Manhattan Bank Sucks.* It targets mortgages, credit cards and customer service. A bulletin board allows customers and ex-employees to gripe about every service Chase provides. The site also provides links to news stories about how *Chase's 'right relationship' started with the Nazis during W.W.II* and how *corruption is alive and well at Chase.*

Untied.com

A mistype of united.com (for those looking for United Airlines) leads to untied.com, a self-defined whistleblower and complaint site created by anti-fans of United Airlines. Although it hasn't been updated since March of 2008, this site is still available to the world as a clearinghouse for passenger complaints directed at the customer service department at United.

While large corporations can retain firms to provide domain name management, domain name recovery and online brand protection, small companies are often dealt blows from which they cannot recover. Repeating what I said earlier about the importance of owning your own real estate, you must own not only your name but also the negative versions that could be associated with your name, company or brands. While the thought of having websites built to target your business can be ominous, there is actually a greater threat. There are hundreds of general-purpose complaint sites that have very high authority with search engine algorithms and they work daily to keep it that way.

General Complaint Sites

While eating lunch, a former employee or competitor can post dozens of complaints about you or your business from any smart phone. These general complaint sites have logged literally millions of baseless complaints bashing companies, products, employees, professionals and it is all perfectly legal. There are so many complaint sites that Yahoo! has created a separate directory for them, posting everything from hard core consumer activism and anti-corporate back lashing content to personal revenge and fictitious claims. Not familiar with these sites? Here is just a small sampling of what is out there.

- a380reviews.com
- abusivemen.com
- advertisementcomplaints.com
- alternativemedicinecomplaints.com
- anotherreview.com
- auction-complaints.com
- autofinancingcomplaints.com
- autorepaircomplaints.com
- BadDeals.com
- bankerreviews.com
- beautysaloncomplaints.com
- Blog Post Removal
- Bustathief.com
- campingcomplaints.com
- Canyoutrustthem.com
- catchacheater.com
- childcarecomplaints.com
- cleaningcomplaints.com
- clientstory.com

- codeprofile.com
- communicationcomplaints.com
- ComplaintCenter.com
- Complaintnow.com
- Complaints.com
- Complaintsboard.com
- conreviews.com
- consultingcomplaints.com
- ConsumerAffairs.com
- consumerfraudreporting.org
- ConsumerWebWatch.org
- ConsumerXchange.org
- corpreviews.com
- cosmeticcomplaints.com
- creditcard-complaints.com
- cruise-complaints.com
- customer-story.com
- cutesig.com
- days-inn.hotel-complaints.com
- debtservicecomplaints.com
- directlendercomplaints.com
- drugscomplaints.com
- drycleanercomplaints.com
- electronicscomplaints.com
- emergencyservicecomplaints.com
- emohome.com
- employmentcomplaints.com
- entertainmentcomplaints.com
- expedia.hotel-complaints.com
- fightadware.com

- financecomplaints.com
- financingreviews.com
- fitnesscomplaints.com
- fraudwatchers.com
- freeprincess.com
- geo-leo-elias.net
- GetSatisfaction.com
- globalmobileadvertising.com
- grocerycomplaints.com
- hardwarecomplaints.com
- harrahs.hotel-complaints.com
- healthrunner.com
- hithealth.com
- hospital-complaints.com
- hotel-complaints.com
- hotwire.hotel-complaints.com
- hummingbird-house.hotel-complaints.com
- infidelitystories.com
- infidelitytestamonials.com
- installercomplaints.com
- intownsuites.hotel-complaints.com
- investmentcomplaints.com
- iripoff.com
- kosherservice.com
- laundrycomplaints.com
- loancomplaints.com
- marinacomplaints.com
- marriott-international.hotel-complaints.com
- medicalcentercomplaints.com
- medicalequipmentcomplaints.com

- mgm-mirage-grand.hotel-complaints.com
- mortgagebroker-complaints.com
- movingscam.com
- movingstoragecomplaints.com
- My3Cents.com
- onlineinfidelitybook.com
- phoneownerinfo.com
- picsedit.com
- picseditor.com
- Pissed.com
- PissedConsumer.com
- Pissedoff.com
- pixeditor.com
- PlanetFeedback.com
- pleasedconsumer.com
- priceline.hotel-complaints.com
- productreviews911.com
- professionalcomplaints.com
- protecttheconsumer.com
- rate-a-girl.com
- repaircomplaints.com
- resortcomplaints.com
- restaurant-complaints.com
- restaurant-complaints.com
- Ripoff.com
- Ripoffonline.com
- Ripoffreport.com
- Scam.com
- Scamclub.com
- school complaints.com

- screwedcentral.com
- sears.laundrycomplaints.com
- shopperstory.com
- Sitejabber.com
- spa-complaints.com
- special-t-travel.hotel-complaints.com
- store-complaints.com
- stylehot.com
- thebankreviews.com
- thebrokerreviews.com
- theservicereviews.com
- TheSqueakyWheel.com
- tourismcomplaints.com
- tutorcomplaints.com
- tutorreviews.com
- upsetclient.com
- upsetconsumer.com
- upsetshopper.com
- vendorcomplaints.com
- veterinarycomplaints.com
- vocalist.org.uk
- whocallsme.com
- womansaversblog.com
- writecomplaint.com
- datingpsychos.com
- dontdatehimgirl.com

As Dr. Wagner learned the hard way, legal action is next to impossible against those who write defaming material or the site that hosts that material. In a highly publicized defamation suit, Nemet Chevrolet of

Jamaica, New York filed suit against ConsumerAffairs.com. Franchised car dealer Thomas Nemet listed in the lawsuit seven examples of complaints placed on the site, including the following posting:

> *"We were trying to lease a car. Unfortunately, we got too excited so they took advantage by adding a lot of extras to the car without informing us."*

A federal court threw out the defamation suit against ConsumerAffairs. com. The Nemet case has been appealed; however, the decisions of the lower courts in favor of ConsumerAffairs.com and against Nemet continue to be upheld. David Johnson of InternetCommerceLaw.com offers this:

> *The dominant understanding among U.S. Circuit Courts is that the Communications Decency Act is an immunity statute that* **protects an ISP (internet service provider) from any kind of civil suit for publishing information from a third party.**

In other words, the ISP is protected and you are not. And while legal recourse against the person who wrote the material may be possible, it is again unlikely due to the anonymity of such postings.[27] [28]

An example of how these sites are protected is found in the small print of a complaint site that claims to serve the consumer. While the site is less than three years old, there are already thousands of complaints posted. Notice the defensive strategy taken in their terms and conditions. The first seven sections explain that access to the site is at the reader's risk and that there is no liability accepted by the website for what is posted. Sections eight through ten state:

8. Complaints and accounts of incidents posted on [this website] are not complaints by the creators or owners of the site.

9. [This website] merely provides a posting system and settlement option so each claim can be resolved.

10. We are not responsible for the accuracy or truthfulness of advice or information or data provided online and disclaim any responsibility for the consequences of acting on such information.

One upside is that the website does make the following clear:

You can personally be held legally liable for what you say or do online. For example, you can be held accountable for defamatory comments, threats and statements that are illegal or fraudulent.

All you have to do is conclusively determine exactly *who* wrote *what* and from *where*, that's all. Almost without exception, a majority of these complaint sites present as slander sites and provide little real value. But positioning themselves as third party content sites that do not actually create the content excludes them from responsibility to authenticate the truth or accuracy of any posted claims. While reason would suggest that there must be a direct way through the courts to demand these sites be taken down or else required to validate claims like the Better Business Bureau and Consumer Affairs do, I don't believe that this type of accountability will be consistently required anytime soon.

So what is a person to do? First, don't live in denial. If you don't have a computer at home and you don't feel comfortable using the one at work, go to the library, borrow a computer, or use your friend's cell phone to check out your own search results. Search your name(s) and your business name in all its forms. Knowledge is power.

Second, do the homework. Buy a book, research the Internet, or call a professional that understands these issues and can educate you. I frequently speak with people who have tried to solve complaint site violations on their own. The problem with this approach is that for obvious reasons the person is too emotional, too close to the sting of the complaint. Professionals in the area of online reputation have no skin in the game and can offer an objective eye. A controlled, measured response over time yields results, screaming does not.

Finally, refer back to the "Ten Rules of Complaint Sites." Desperation leads people to poor choices, even when they are executives in high profile businesses. Don't forget that it's possible to go from a bad situation to a courtroom very quickly. As an example, the President of plastic surgery practice Lifestyle Lift directed an employee via a company email to *Put your wig and skirt on and tell them about the great experience you had.* Lifestyle Lift's pending lawsuit against the complaint site RealSelf.com, was followed by a suit against Lifestyle Lift by RealSelf.com for the phony postings. Both suits were settled out of court. These illegal actions cost Lifestyle Lift over $300,000.

The Why

As we wrap up this chapter, you may be wondering why someone would establish a complaint site on the Internet. It's simple. Most complaint sites offer advertising throughout their website. Sites that create consistent web traffic can actually sell advertising space and generate recurring income. The larger the site becomes, the more traffic is attracted and thus the more "eyeballs" see the advertising. What a business plan! Grow a big site with lots of complaints and unsubstantiated slander, run it overseas out of a virtual office with no real employees and low overhead, create lots of traffic and you will reap a steady stream of income.

As of the writing of this book we see no end in sight to these complaint sites. Your best defense is to get educated about, and engaged with, how you are presented on the Internet. No one will ever be more interested in defending and protecting your name than you are. You simply cannot sit back and hope that you are not the next target.

If there was one positive result from Dr. Wagner's nightmare, it was that he was rocked out of Internet apathy. Dr. Wagner learned about search results, search engines, cyberlaw, page rankings, Internet Service Providers and he acquired the latest in modern technology and software—the salesman saw him coming! These days as he sits in his office with the glow of a twenty-one inch monitor reflecting off his glasses, he knows there are resources that exist solely to alleviate pain such as his. There *are* actions that can be taken to offset the damage his reputation suffered.

The story does have a fairly happy ending. While Dr. Wagner will never know the full impact that this ordeal had on his dental practice, he has gained a new respect for the power of a keyboard and connection to the Internet. He is now actively engaged in his online reputation and has empowered himself to take control of the tools available to influence his virtual identity.

What about *you?*

Five Things to Remember

1. Complaints are never private.

2. Complaints are almost always anonymous.

3. There is no pragmatic legal recourse.

4. Filing a rebuttal can only harm you.

5. Education and action are your only defense.

Chapter 11
Violation Help

All "help" is not helpful.

Years ago, my cousin Jim and I drove from a western Chicago suburb to the Wisconsin Dells, a vacation destination that was only a couple of hours away. In our sights was an adventure that could be had for half a tank of gas and less than $100. We ended up at a sailboat rental dock and realized that adventure was indeed at hand. There was just one small problem—neither one of us had ever actually sailed. The rental agreement required that we affirm our knowledge of jibbing, rigging, rudders and booms; of course we replied yes! Our goal was to hit the water *ASAP*, plus we knew we could figure it out. After all, how hard could wind be?

Catching big wind wasn't a big deal. However, we misjudged the challenges of sailing. Turning was, ummm… an *issue*. Jim, being older and more experienced (he owned a power boat) was at the helm and I was relegated to handling the ropes—I mean, the lines. As we "came about" and the sail caught wind on the opposite side of the sail, the boom quickly swung to the other side of the boat and an unexpected impact with my head caught me off guard. All of a sudden I found myself treading water *(Who needs a life jacket? It might mess up my tan…)* with my cousin laughing hysterically as he sailed past me. Bobbing up and down in the water, it became clear that there was more to sailing than we wanted to admit.

Hold that thought.

Sam Tanner was a savvy businessman. His business was located in the West, in a city that requires street smarts to survive. And street-smart entrepreneur he was, winning many more times than he had lost. But business acumen was no match for a former employee who had been fired for poor job performance and decided to get even by posting slander on the Internet.

Like most people we have worked with, Sam Tanner found us through our website. In the initial conversation, he asked us three basic questions. *How do you do it? How fast can it be done? How much does it cost?* As we talked further, it was pretty easy to determine that his previous business successes had not prepared him for the voyage he was about to take.

As with all of our clients, we try to make it clear that we are not the biggest firm and that we are not the least expensive. After Sam reviewed our proposal, he determined that we were a good fit. We are fortunate in finding many clients that agree we suit their needs and Sam was one of them.

Normally, as we begin pre-production for a project, we purchase domain names on behalf of a client and Sam Tanner was no different. He had mentioned in an early conversation that he had originally talked to another company that said they could do it faster and cheaper than we could, but he was happy with his decision to hire us. When asked how far his conversations had progressed with the other company, he admitted they had sent him a contract but it was quite poorly written and that's when he decided to go with us.

When Sam initially disclosed this conversation, his words "made my antenna quiver." In other words, something in my gut did not feel right and my internal antenna was on alert. As we continued to work through the process of securing the URLs for Sam's name my concerns were validated. Sam Tanner's name and many extensions of his name had been purchased—all within the past week.

Uh-oh.

Now let me tie these two stories together.

Within online reputation management (ORM) there are reputable service providers, but as with any other emerging industry there are those who are in it only to make fast money. As we have reviewed the work of our peers we appreciate how progressive our industry has become in a short period of time but have noted that there is a dangerous, shadow side as well.

A *no money down, pay us when we get the job done* offer had prompted Sam Tanner's initial call to the other company. Promises of quick results and a price that was far less than Sam thought it might be drew out his implied commitment, and that was enough—so they said—to quickly secure not only the URLs associated with Sam's name, but also more than 100 social and profile sites. Now Sam could not own his own "real estate." He called the other company, explaining that there had been a misunderstanding and that he had not signed the agreement. His appeals fell on deaf ears. The company had been engaged to provide services and Sam owed them fees—*large fees.*

Before I continue, let me make a general statement: Most people that contact us do not understand how Search Engine Reputation Management (SERM) works. They *do* know two things, they have been damaged by online content and it is impacting their life. Understandably, their primary goal is for quick relief from the pain. However, a situation can actually become worse if it is approached recklessly. In the case of

Sam Tanner, he felt confident that he knew all about jibbing, rigging, turning and—most importantly—the boom. But like me in the rented sailboat, Sam quickly found himself treading water without a life jacket and trying to process what had happened.

Screaming extortion accomplished nothing. *After all, who could he complain to?*

As we evaluated the situation, it became apparent that the cost and timeline involved in reaching the target would need to be expanded considerably. And while his story probably does not represent the experience of most people, I do believe that there are hundreds of offshore companies attempting to enter the market in the U.S. — not all of which are solid.

Without going into all the gory details, I can tell you that this street smart entrepreneur ended up sending a cashier's check for thousands of dollars in exchange for the other company's agreement to suspend their activity and sign over the URLs that represented his virtual person.

Again, I want to repeat what I said earlier: There are many quality service providers engaged in online reputation management. However, as with any other product or service, a *Buyer Beware* perspective is best. Educating yourself is critical when dealing with your online reputation. Going back to my sailing story, Jim and I had not taken the time to learn the basic, important details about how to manage the boat. The same was true for Sam Tanner. And all three of us suffered the consequences.

One common misunderstanding regarding services that relate to search engine results is the various acronyms that are used when discussing services. So that we have a clear understanding of what is needed to protect and rehabilitate your online search results, let me provide a basic explanation for the two key sets of services that companies like ours provide.

A Search Engine Optimization (SEO) company focuses predominantly on the promotion of a single web site. Good SEO companies can elevate the ranking of a website on search engines to the very top for a specific search term (keyword). SEO is a primarily a tool for businesses that want to be found easily when certain keywords are searched for either on a local or a national level. SEO companies take static space on the Internet and bring it to front-page visibility on the Web. It's like the difference between advertising on a billboard in the desert and having Times Square visibility. *No comparison.* The idea is to build a dominant online presence for a website.

Published reports suggest that 88% of all click-through traffic for businesses online go to the top three non-paid listings. You can understand then why a business would retain SEO services to position their page rank high for various search terms. But what happens when content is created and promoted about a person or company that is not under that person/company's control? Suppose that the content shows false information that is damaging, embarrassing and hurtful—what then? That's where companies dedicated to online reputation management come into play.

These service companies are referred to as Search Engine Reputation Management (SERM) firms. (Another acronym you may see is ORM or Online Reputation Management.) SERM helps people like those you have read about in this book. SERM evaluates negative content, tracks comments, postings and opinions online and builds and executes strategies designed to remove, alter or otherwise influence that content and the ranking of specific targeted slander and complaint sites. In short, SERM companies methodically work to counteract negative postings on behalf of clients. The end result is that the client's good name is preserved and/or restored. While there are similarities, SERM companies and SEO companies require different disciplines, tools and approaches to accomplish quite different goals.

The goal of SEO is to increase traffic to a specific website. For instance, if a shopper is looking for athletic shoes, the goal of Nike would be to employ SEO techniques to improve the chance that when the term "athletic shoes" is searched, the shopper will find Nike.com in the first position on page one. SEO companies use techniques such as backlinks, site optimization and Nike's popularity on sites like Facebook and Twitter to improve the value or *authority* that Nike.com has with the search engine algorithms. SERM uses websites, blogs, forums, social profile sites and content syndication to promote organic, transparent information about a client. This content is built to rank well with search engines and develop strong rankings for this new content. So a company uses SEO services to drive traffic to their specific site, but when viewers are suddenly exposed to a snarl of negative comments, litigation, unfair reviews or online slander, a SERM company will be engaged to re-establish their online reputation.

Many times our clients have initially retained an SEO firm for online marketing purposes prior to contacting us for assistance with SERM. These relationships work in tandem since the objectives complement each other well—think of it as *yin* and *yang*. While SEO efforts advance a site toward the top of search results, SERM works to suppress results that are already ranking highly for a keyword and need to be pushed down. While the outcome appears somewhat similar, the tools, links and strategies are almost always different.

So what else is important to know before you begin to "sail?" Just as my cousin and I didn't ask the right questions, Sam Tanner failed to ask some very important questions before he made a verbal commitment. Because we live in a world of portable technology, phantom phone numbers and identities that may be difficult to verify, the more information that can be validated about a vendor you are considering, the better off you will be.

As a simple beginning, you might determine if the company has a street address. Searching their address in Google Maps will allow you to determine if the location is in a business park, a residence, or a retail location like The UPS Store. Should you not receive the services you contracted for and phone calls and email go unanswered, having an address where mail can be successfully delivered may be of help.

Is the firm a member of any trade or civic organization such as the Chamber of Commerce or Better Business Bureau? Most of the time, such organizations go through a vetting process that validates the viability of a perspective member company. The Better Business Bureau will also validate incorporation information, interview officers and many times make an on-site visit to the office. It is not foolproof, but it is an objective third party evaluation.

Then there is always the issue of payment for services. If services are aggressively offered for free initially, if demand is made for a cashier's check, Moneygram, Western Union, PayPal, or immediate bank transfer, or if a company cannot process a credit card payment through a conventional credit card processor, your antenna might begin to quiver. Yes, PayPal and Google offer payment processing for Visa and MasterCard, but your recourse may be more limited. Traditional bank processing offers you certain recovery abilities if specific services *agreed to in writing* are not delivered. These abilities may not be available through other forms of payment.

And let me add one additional thought relating to payment for SERM services—beware of *absolute* guarantees relating to specific search engine results being achieved. SERM and ORM are almost always provided on a "best efforts" basis, and absent a very specific detailed and well-defined written guarantee, you will always be dependent on the integrity of the company you have hired. The word "guarantee" can mean different things to different companies, so get as much clarification as possible.

One final thought concerning online reputation services. It is essential that you as the client discuss your assumptions regarding results. You may have certain expectations for the project that can never be met. Even if the slander is suppressed, the end result could leave you with inferior search results for your name that do not meet your quality expectations. In other words, you might end up with your slander being suppressed by what most people would consider as spam sites. This is not totally the vendor's error. They have been retained to suppress the negative posting, not create a quality marketing effort for you. But SERM companies should be able to offer services that both suppress and promote *when the project is defined clearly up front.*

Most companies work hard to meet client expectations. It is important that you listen well, ask good questions and stay involved in the project. You should always review and approve your content before it is used. You should review and approve websites before they go live. You should expect your email and phone calls to be returned and you should expect to be able to actually *find* the company you have hired if there is a problem.

With that said, as this book has suggested, there are many things that you can do on your own to protect yourself, your family and your business. If you have less experience with the Internet, if you use it only for email, a little social interaction, or to keep up with the news, don't be intimidated. One of the truly positive aspects of the Internet is access to a plethora of educational information, and it's right at your fingertips. There are dozens of "how to" videos on sites like youtube.com. There are free webinars, others that charge a nominal fee, and they will walk you through the steps necessary to build your online defense. You will also find many helpful books and resources on sites like amazon.com.

A final consideration is *time.* In becoming aware of the level of exposure you may have, the tendency will be to feel an urgency to *fix everything now.* For some, there is indeed an immediate need because online slander and misinformation is hurting business, employment opportunities or causing embarrassment with family, peers and friends. But for most people, this book will serve to create a heightened sense of awareness and the need to *begin* a proactive process.

As you create online sites, write and post relevant content and consistently review the information found about you online, the process will become more familiar to you. Take your time, read and learn, and then act. You *can* control your online identity and not be Violated Online.

Five Things to Remember

1. Remember that some companies offering to help you may actually be more focused on "helping" themselves.

2. There is a major difference between an SEO and SERM Company.

3. Evaluate any company you hire so that you have confidence in them.

4. Educating yourself is essential and there should be no assumptions.

5. Set clear expectations defining results for your project.

Appendix One
Social Media Guide

For those of you that want to take additional steps to secure your identity online, I am providing a list of social sites as found on SEOmoz.com. You should attempt to secure your name on each of these sites. Doing so helps to insure that no one else can claim it as his or her identity. You will find that, in some cases, "your" name has already been claimed by someone else; don't panic. In most cases there are other people in the world with the same name as you. If this happens, attempt to secure your first+middle+last name or your nickname. Any real estate claimed can only be of positive benefit.

Name	URL	Category
Wikipedia	http://www.wikipedia.org/	Wikis
YouTube	http://www.youtube.com/	Video
StumbleUpon	http://www.stumbleupon.com/	Social Tagging
Technorati	http://technorati.com/	Social Tagging
Stylehive	http://www.stylehive.com/	Social Tagging
Del.icio.us	http://delicious.com/	Social News / Tagging
Yahoo! Meme	http://meme.yahoo.com/home/	Social News / Bookmarking
Digg	http://digg.com/	Social News
Ning	http://www.ning.com	Social Networking
Plaxo	http://www.plaxo.com/	Social Networking
Hi5	http://hi5.com/	Social Networking
Orkut	http://www.orkut.com/Signup	Social Networking
Friendster	http://www.friendster.com/	Social Networking

Bebo	http://www.bebo.com/c/site/index	Social Networking
Plurk	http://www.plurk.com/	Social Networking
Viadeo	http://www.viadeo.com/en/connexion/	Social Networking
Facebook	http://www.facebook.com/home.php	Social Networking
MySpace	http://www.myspace.com/	Social Networking
Google Profile	http://www.google.com/profiles	Social Networking
MyBlogLog	http://www.mybloglog.com/	Social Networking
Yelp	http://www.yelp.com/	Reviews
Amazon	http://www.amazon.com/	Retail
LinkedIn	http://www.linkedin.com/	Professional Networking
SlideShare	http://www.slideshare.net/	Presentation Sharing
Flickr	http://www.flickr.com/	Photo Sharing
Last.fm	http://www.last.fm/	Music
Meetup	http://www.meetup.com/	Events
Eventful	http://eventful.com/	Events
Upcoming	http://upcoming.yahoo.com/	Events
TeachStreet	http://www.teachstreet.com/	Education
Epinions	http://www.epinions.com/	Consumer Reviews
IMDb Pro	http://www.imdb.com/	Community
BuddyTV	http://www.buddytv.com	Community
Barnes and Noble	https://cart2.barnesandnoble.com/account/op.asp?x=39162108	Community
Multiply	http://multiply.com/	Community
Hunch	http://www.hunch.com/	Community
Tribe.net	http://www.tribe.net/welcome	Community
WikiHow	http://www.wikihow.com/Main-Page	Wikis
WetPaint	http://www.wetpaint.com/	Wikis
Magnify	http://www.magnify.net/	Video
Scribd	http://www.scribd.com/	Social Publishing
Faves	http://faves.com/home	Social News / Bookmarking
Faves	http://faves.com/home	Social News / Bookmarking
Yahoo! Buzz	http://buzz.yahoo.com/	Social News
NowPublic	http://www.nowpublic.com/	Social News
HubSpot	http://www.hubspot.com/	Social News
Hacker News	http://news.ycombinator.com/	Social News
Newsvine	http://www.newsvine.com/	Social News
Propeller	http://www.propeller.com/	Social News
Jumptags	http://www.jumptags.com/	Social News
Plime	http://www.plime.com/	Social News
Folkd	http://www.folkd.com/	Social News
Simpy	http://www.simpy.com/	Social News
ShoutWire	http://shoutwire.com/	Social News
Meneame	http://meneame.net/	Social News
Linkinn	http://www.linkinn.com/	Social News

DotNetKicks	http://dotnetkicks.com/default.aspx	Social News
coRank	http://www.corank.com/	Social News
DNHour	http://www.dnhour.com/	Social News
CoMagz	http://www.comagz.com/	Social News
Mister Wong	http://www.mister-wong.com/	Social Bookmarking
BibSonomy	http://www.bibsonomy.org/	Social Bookmarking
Connectedy	http://www.connectedy.com/	Social Bookmarking
Slashdot	http://slashdot.org/	News Aggregator
Techmeme	http://www.techmeme.com/	News Aggregator
Yahoo! Picks	http://picks.yahoo.com/	News
Fanpop	http://www.fanpop.com/	Fan Site
Adobe Showcase	http://www.adobe.com/cfusion/showcase/index.cfm	Editorially Chosen Content
AskMen	http://ca.askmen.com/media_kit/suggest/index.html	Editorially Chosen Content
CSS Beauty	http://www.cssbeauty.com/	Editorially Chosen Content
CSS Vault	http://cssvault.com/	Editorially Chosen Content
InternetMosaic	http://internetmosaic.com/	Content Submission
StyleHive	http://www.stylehive.com/	Community
Twitter	http://twitter.com/	Community
Kaboodle	http://www.kaboodle.com/	Community
Fark	http://www.fark.com/	Community
ma.gnolia	http://ma.gnolia.com/	Community
Bestuff	http://bestuff.com/	Bookmarking
43places	http://www.43places.com	Bookmarking
Jaiku	http://www.jaiku.com/	Bookmarking
Poseterous	http://posterous.com/	Blogging / Sharing
Metafilter	http://www.metafilter.com/	Blogging / Community
Diigo	http://www.diigo.com/	Social News / Bookmarking
Tweako	http://www.tweako.com/	Social News / Bookmarking
Reddit	http://www.reddit.com	Social News
ShowHype	http://showhype.com/	Social News
TreeHugger	http://www.treehugger.com/	Social News
Ballhype	http://ballhype.com/	Social News
Mixx	http://www.mixx.com/	Social News
Sphinn	http://sphinn.com/	Social News
Buzzflash	http://www.buzzflash.com/	Social News
IndianPad	http://www.indianpad.com/	Social News
Socialogs	http://socialogs.com/	Social News
Blogs4god	http://www.blogs4god.com/	Social News
ScoreGuru	http://scoreguru.com/	Social News
Xanga	http://www.xanga.com/	Social Networking and Blogging
CouchSurfing	http://www.couchsurfing.org/	Social Networking
DriverSide	http://www.driverside.com/	Social Networking

Pixel Groovy	http://www.pixelgroovy.com/	Social Directory
Searchles	http://www.searchles.com/	Social Bookmarking
A1 Webmarks	http://www.a1-webmarks.com/	Social Bookmarking
Zlitt	http://www.zlitt.com/	Social Bookmarking
Curiobot	http://curiobot.net/	Shopping
DeviantArt	http://www.deviantart.com/	Self-publishing, Social Networking
23	http://www.23hq.com/	Photo sharing
Care2	http://www.care2.com/	Philanthropy
ChipIn	http://www.chipin.com/	Philanthropy
EzineArticles	http://ezinearticles.com/	News Aggregator
Small Business Brief	http://www.smallbusinessbrief.com/index.php	News
Value Investing News	http://www.valueinvestingnews.com/	News
RealEstateVoices	http://www.realestatevoices.com/	News
My Link Vault	http://www.mylinkvault.com/	Link Directory
[adult swim]	http://www.adultswim.com/	Fan Site
Dfinitive	http://dfinitive.com/	Directory / Bookmarking
Squidoo	http://www.squidoo.com/	Community
Get Satisfaction	http://getsatisfaction.com/	Community
MotoSport	http://www.motosport.com/	Community
TripIt	http://www.tripit.com/	Community
SocialPicks	http://www.socialpicks.com/	Community
Social Media Club	http://www.socialmediaclub.org/	Community
Spotback	http://spotback.com/	Bookmarking
memFrag	http://www.memfrag.com/	Bookmarking
Blogger	https://www.blogger.com/start	Blogging Software / Host
Wordpress	http://wordpress.org/showcase/	Blogging Software / Host
Tumblr	http://www.tumblr.com/	Blogging Software / Host
Blogsome	http://www.blogsome.com/	Blogging Software / Host

Appendix Two
Section 230 of the Communications Decency Act

Source: Wikipedia

Section 230 of the Communications Decency Act of 1996 (a common name for Title V of the Telecommunications Act of 1996) is a landmark piece of Internet legislation in the United States, codified at 47 U.S.C. § 230. Section 230(c)(1) provides immunity from liability for providers and users of an "interactive computer service" who publish information provided by others: *No provider or user of an interactive computer service shall be treated as the publisher or speaker of any information provided by another information content provider.*

In analyzing the availability of the immunity offered by this provision, courts generally apply a three-prong test. A defendant must satisfy each of the three prongs to gain the benefit of the immunity:

1. The defendant must be a "provider or user" of an "interactive computer service."
2. The cause of action asserted by the plaintiff must "treat" the defendant "as the publisher or speaker" of the harmful information at issue.
3. The information must be "provided by another information content provider," i.e., the defendant must not be the "information content provider" of the harmful information at issue.

History

Section 230 of the Communications Decency Act was not part of the original Senate legislation, but was added in conference with the House of Representatives, where it had been separately introduced by Representatives Chris Cox (R-CA) and Ron Wyden (D-OR) as the Internet Freedom and Family Empowerment Act and passed by a near-unanimous vote on the floor. Unlike the more controversial anti-indecency provisions which were later ruled unconstitutional, this portion of the Act remains in force, and enhances free speech by making it unnecessary for ISPs and other service providers to unduly restrict customers' actions for fear of being found legally liable for customers' conduct. The act was passed in part in reaction to the 1995 decision in *Stratton Oakmont, Inc. v. Prodigy Services Co.*,[1] which suggested that service providers who assumed an editorial role with regard to customer content, thus became publishers, and legally responsible for libel and other torts committed by customers. This act was passed to specifically enhance service providers' ability to delete or otherwise monitor content without themselves becoming publishers.

In *Zeran v. America Online, Inc.*, the Court notes that "Congress enacted § 230 to remove the disincentives to self-regulation created by the *Stratton Oakmont* decision. Under that court's holding, computer service providers who regulated the dissemination of offensive material on their services risked subjecting themselves to liability, because such regulation cast the service provider in the role of a publisher. Fearing that the specter of liability would therefore deter service providers from blocking and screening offensive material, Congress enacted § 230's broad immunity "to remove disincentives for the development and utilization of blocking and filtering technologies that empower parents to restrict their children's access to objectionable or inappropriate online material." In addition, *Zeran* notes "the amount of information communicated via interactive computer services is...staggering. The specter of tort liability in an area of such prolific speech would have an obviously chilling effect. It would be impossible for service providers to screen each of their millions of postings for possible problems. Faced with potential liability for each message republished by their services, interactive computer service providers might choose to severely restrict the number and type of messages posted. Congress considered the weight of the speech interests implicated and chose to immunize service providers to avoid any such restrictive effect."

Limits

Section 230's coverage is not complete: it excepts federal criminal liability and intellectual property law. 47 U.S.C. §§ 230(e)(1) (criminal) and (e)(2) (intellectual property); see also *Gucci America, Inc. v. Hall & Associates*, 135 F. Supp. 2d 409 (S.D.N.Y. 2001) (no immunity for contributory liability for trademark infringement). In *Perfect 10, Inc. v. CCBill LLC*, 481 F.3d 751 (9th Cir. Mar. 29, 2007; amended opinion issued May 31, 2007) the Court of Appeals ruled that the exception for intellectual property law applies only to federal intellectual property law, reversing a district court ruling that the exception applies to state right of publicity claims. *Cf. Carfano*, 339 F.3d 1119 (dismissing, inter alia, right of publicity claim under Section 230 without discussion), *but see Doe v. Friendfinder Network, Inc.*, 540 F.Supp.2d 288 (D.N.H. 2008) (230 does not immunize against state IP claims, including right of publicity claims). The *Friendfinder* court specifically discussed and rejected the Ninth Circuit's reading of "intellectual property law" in *CCBill* and held that the immunity does not reach state right of publicity claims.

Section 230 is controversial because several courts have interpreted it as providing complete immunity for ISPs with regard to the torts committed by their users over their systems. *See, e.g., Zeran v. AOL*, 129 F.3d 327, 330 (4th Cir. 1997), cert. denied, 524 U.S. 937 (1998), which held that Section 230 "creates a federal immunity to any cause of action that would make service providers liable for information originating with a third-party user of the service." This rule effectively protects online entities, including user-generated content websites, that qualify as a "provider or user" of an "interactive computer service." However some criticize Section 230 for leaving victims with no hope of relief where the true tortfeasors cannot be identified or are judgment proof.

For example, the plaintiff in Zeran was clearly defamed by an unidentified user of AOL's bulletin board, but was unable to bring suit against the original poster due to missing records. Since Section 230 barred Zeran from obtaining damages from AOL, he obtained no redress for the harms the messages caused, including death threats that required the involvement of the FBI.

1. Court Decisions on Section 230

2. Defamatory information

- *Zeran v. AOL*, 129 F.3d 327 (4th Cir. 1997).[2]
Immunity was **upheld** against claims that AOL unreasonably delayed in removing defamatory messages posted by third party, failed to post retractions, and failed to screen for similar postings.
- *Blumenthal v. Drudge*, 992 F. Supp. 44, 49-53 (D.D.C. 1998).[3]
The court **upheld** AOL's immunity from liability for defamation. AOL's agreement with the contractor allowing AOL to modify or remove such content did not make AOL the "information content provider" because the content was created by an independent contractor. The Court noted that Congress made a policy choice by "providing immunity even where the interactive service provider has an active, even aggressive role in making available content prepared by others."
- *Carafano v. Metrosplash.com*, 339 F.3d 1119 (9th Cir. 2003).[4]
The court **upheld** immunity for an Internet dating service provider from liability stemming from third party's submission of false profile. The plaintiff, Carafano, claimed the false profile defamed her, but because the content was created by a third party, the website was immune, even though it had provided multiple choice selections to aid profile creation.
- *Batzel v. Smith*, 333 F.3d 1018 (9th Cir. 2003).[5]
Immunity was **upheld** for a website operator for distributing an email to a listserv where the plaintiff claimed the email was defamatory.

Though there was a question as to whether the information provider intended to send the email to the listserv, the Court decided that for determining the liability of the service provider, "the focus should be not on the information provider's intentions or knowledge when transmitting content but, instead, on the service provider's or user's reasonable perception of those intentions or knowledge." The Court found immunity proper "under circumstances in which a reasonable person in the position of the service provider or user would conclude that the information was provided for publication on the Internet or other 'interactive computer service.'"

- *Green v. AOL*, 318 F.3d 465 (3rd Cir. 2003).[6]

The court **upheld** immunity for AOL against allegations of negligence. Green claimed AOL failed to adequately police its services and allowed third parties to defame him and inflict intentional emotional distress. The court rejected these arguments because holding AOL negligent in promulgating harmful content would be equivalent to holding AOL "liable for decisions relating to the monitoring, screening, and deletion of content from its network -- actions quintessentially related to a publisher's role."

- *Barrett v. Rosenthal*, 40 Cal. 4th 33 (2006).[7]

Immunity was **upheld** for an individual internet user from liability for republication of defamatory statement on a listserv. The court found the defendant to be a "user of interactive computer services" and thus immune from liability for posting information passed to her by the author.

- *MCW, Inc. v. badbusinessbureau.com(RipOff Report/Ed Magedson/ XCENTRIC Ventures LLC)* 2004 WL 833595, No. Civ.A.3:02-CV-2727-G, (N.D. Tex. April 19, 2004).[8]

The court **rejected** the defendant's motion to dismiss on the grounds of Section 230 immunity, ruling that the plaintiff's allegations that the defendants wrote disparaging report titles and headings, and themselves wrote disparaging editorial messages about the plaintiff, rendered them information content providers. The Web site, www.badbusinessbureau.

com, allows users to upload "reports" containing complaints about businesses they have dealt with.

- *Hy Cite Corp. v. badbusinessbureau.com (RipOff Report/Ed Magedson/XCENTRIC Ventures LLC)*, 418 F. Supp. 2d 1142 (D. Ariz. 2005).[9]

The court **rejected** immunity and found the defendant was an "information content provider" under Section 230 using much of the same reasoning as the *MCW* case.

3. False information

- *Gentry v. eBay, Inc.*, 99 Cal. App. 4th 816, 830 (2002).[10]

eBay's immunity was **upheld** for claims based on forged autograph sports items purchased on the auction site.

- *Ben Ezra, Weinstein & Co. v. America Online*, 206 F.3d 980, 984-985 (10th Cir. 2000), cert. denied, 531 U.S. 824 (2000).[11]

Immunity for AOL was **upheld** against liability for a user's posting of incorrect stock information.

- *Goddard v. Google, Inc.*, C 08-2738 JF (PVT), 2008 WL 5245490, 2008 U.S. Dist. LEXIS 101890 (N.D. Cal. Dec. 17, 2008).[12]

Immunity **upheld** against claims of fraud and money laundering. Google was not responsible for misleading advertising created by third parties who bought space on Google's pages. The court found the creative pleading of money laundering did not cause the case to fall into the crime exception to Section 230 immunity.

- *Milgram v. Orbitz Worldwide, LLC*, ESX-C-142-09 (N.J. Super. Ct. Aug. 26, 2010).[13]

Immunity for Orbitz and CheapTickets was **upheld** for claims based on fraudulent ticket listings entered by third parties on ticket resale marketplaces.

4. Sexually explicit content and minors

- *Doe v. America Online*, 783 So. 2d 1010, 1013-1017 (Fl. 2001),[14]
cert. denied, 122 S.Ct. 208 (2000)
The court **upheld** immunity against state claims of negligence based on
"chat room marketing" of obscene photographs of minor by a third party.
- *Kathleen R. v. City of Livermore*, 87 Cal. App. 4th 684, 692 (2001)[15]
The California Court of Appeal **upheld** the immunity of a city from
claims of waste of public funds, nuisance, premises liability, and denial of
substantive due process. The plaintiff's child downloaded pornography
from a public library's computers which did not restrict access to minors.
The court found the library was not responsible for the content of the
internet and explicitly found that section 230(c)(1) immunity covers
governmental entities and taxpayer causes of action.
- *Doe v. MySpace*, 528 F.3d 413 (5th Cir. 2008) [16]
The court **upheld** immunity for a social networking site from negligence
and gross negligence liability for failing to institute safety measures to
protect minors and failure to institute policies relating to age verification.
The Does' daughter had lied about her age and communicated over
MySpace with a man who later sexually assaulted her. In the court's
view, the Does' allegations, were "merely another way of claiming that
MySpace was liable for publishing the communications."
- *Dart v. Craigslist, Inc.*, 665 F. Supp. 2d 961 (N.D. Ill. Oct. 20, 2009)[17]
The court **upheld** immunity for Craigslist against a county sheriff's claims
that its "erotic services" section constituted a public nuisance because it
caused or induced prostitution.

5. Discriminatory housing ads

- *Chicago Lawyers' Committee For Civil Rights Under Law, Inc. v.
Craigslist, Inc.* 519 F.3d 666 (7th Cir. 2008).[18]
The court **upheld** immunity for Craigslist against Fair Housing Act
claims based on discriminatory statements in postings on the classifieds
website by third party users.

- *Fair Housing Council of San Fernando Valley v. Roommates.com, LLC*, 521 F.3d 1157 (9th Cir. 2008) (*en banc*).[19]

The Ninth Circuit Court of Appeals *rejected* immunity for the Roommates.com roommate matching service for claims brought under the federal Fair Housing Act[20] and California housing discrimination laws.[21] The court concluded that the manner in which the service elicited information from users concerning their roommate preferences (by having dropdowns specifying gender, presence of children, and sexual orientation), and the manner in which it utilized that information in generating roommate matches (by eliminating profiles that did not match user specifications), the matching service created or developed the information claimed to violate the FHA, and thus was responsible for it as an "information content provider." The court *upheld* immunity for the descriptions posted by users in the "Additional Comments" section because these were entirely created by users.

6. Threats
- Delfino v. *Agilent Technologies*, 145 Cal. App. 4th 790 (2006), cert denied, 128 S. Ct. 98 (2007).
A California Appellate Court unanimously *upheld* immunity from state tort claims arising from an employee's use of the employer's e-mail system to send threatening messages. The court concluded that an employer that provides Internet access to its employees qualifies as a "provider . . . of an interactive service."

Freedom of speech on the Internet
In a 9-0 decision, the Supreme Court extended the full protection of the First Amendment to the Internet in *Reno v. ACLU*, a decision which struck down portions of the 1996 Communications Decency Act, a law intended to outlaw so-called "indecent" online communication (that is, non-obscene material protected by the First Amendment). The court's decision extended the same Constitutional protections given to books, magazines, films, and

spoken expression to materials published on the Internet. Congress tried a second time to regulate the content of the Internet with the Child Online Protection Act (COPA). The Court again ruled that any limitations on the Internet were unconstitutional in American Civil Liberties Union v. Ashcroft (2002).

In *United States v. American Library Association* (2003) the Supreme Court ruled that Congress has the authority to require public schools and libraries receiving e-rate discounts to install filters as a condition of receiving federal funding. The justices said that any First Amendment concerns were addressed by the provisions in the Children's Internet Protection Act that permit adults to ask librarians to disable the filters or unblock individual sites.

(Published on Citizen Media Law Project—http://www.citmedialaw.org)

Immunity for Online Publishers Under the Communications Decency Act

This page provides some background on section 230 of the Communications Decency Act [1] ("Section 230") and highlights the types of claims and online activities it covers as well as the types of activities that might fall outside Section 230's immunity [2] provisions.

For general information on legal liability [3] associated with publishing the content of others, see the section on Publishing the Statements and Content of Others [4] in this guide.

Background on Publisher and Distributor Liability

Under standard common-law principles, a person who publishes a defamatory [5] statement by another bears the same liability for the statement as if he or she had initially created it. Thus, a book publisher or a newspaper publisher can be held liable for anything that appears within its pages. The theory behind this "publisher" liability is that a publisher has the knowledge, opportunity, and ability to exercise editorial control over the content of its publications.

Distributor liability is much more limited. Newsstands, bookstores, and libraries are generally not held liable for the content of the material that they distribute. The concern is that it would be impossible for distributors to read every publication before they sell or distribute it, and that as a result, distributors would engage in excessive self-censorship. In addition, it would be very hard for distributors to know whether something is actionable [6] defamation; after all, speech must be false to be defamatory.

Not surprisingly, the first websites to be sued for defamation based on the statements of others argued that they were merely distributors, and not publishers, of the content on their sites. One of the first such cases was Cubby v. CompuServe, Inc. [7], 776 F.Supp. 135 (S.D.N.Y. 1991). CompuServe provided subscribers with access to over 150 specialty electronic "forums" that were run by third parties. When CompuServe was sued over allegedly defamatory statements that appeared in the "Rumorville" forum, it argued that it should be treated like a distributor because it did not review the contents of the bulletin board before it appeared on CompuServe's site. The court agreed and dismissed the case against CompuServe.

Four years later, a New York state court came to the opposite conclusion when faced with a website that held itself out as a "family friendly" computer network. In Stratton Oakmont v. Prodigy [8], 23 Media L. Rep. 1794 (N.Y. Sup. Ct. 1995), the court held that because Prodigy was exercising editorial control over the messages that appeared on its bulletin boards through its content guidelines and software screening program, Prodigy was more like a "publisher" than a "distributor" and therefore fully liable for all of the content on its site.

The perverse upshot of the *CompuServe* and *Stratton* decisions was that any effort by an online information provider to restrict or edit user-submitted content on its site faced a much higher risk of liability if it failed to eliminate all defamatory material than if it simply didn't try to control or edit the content of third parties at all.

The Communications Decency Act

This prompted Congress to pass the Communications Decency Act [9] in 1996. The Act contains deceptively simple language under the heading "Protection for Good Samaritan blocking and screening of offensive material": *No provider or user of an interactive computer service shall be treated as the publisher or speaker of any information provided by another information content provider.*

Section 230 further provides that "[n]o cause of action may be brought and no liability may be imposed under any State or local law that is inconsistent with this section."

Websites Covered by Section 230

Is an "interactive computer service" some special type of website? No. For purposes of Section 230, an *"interactive computer service" means any information service, system, or access software provider that provides or enables computer access by multiple users to a computer server.*

Most courts have held that through these provisions, Congress granted interactive services of all types, including blogs, forums, and listservs, immunity from tort liability so long as the information is provided by a third party. As a result of Section 230, Internet publishers are treated differently from publishers in print, television, and radio. Let's look at these differences in more detail.

Claims Covered by Section 230

Section 230 has most frequently been applied to bar defamation-based claims. In the typical case, a plaintiff who believes she has been defamed sues both the author of the statement and the website that provided a forum or otherwise passively hosted the material. Courts have held with virtual unanimity that such claims against a website are barred by Section 230. But immunity under Section 230 is not limited to defamation or speech-based torts. Courts have applied Section 230 immunity to bar claims such as invasion of privacy, misappropriation, and most recently in a case brought against MySpace (Doe v. MySpace [10], 474 F.Supp.2d 843 (W.D. Tex. 2007)), a claim asserting that MySpace was negligent for failing to implement age verification procedures and to protect a fourteen-year old from sexual predators. However, Section 230 explicitly exempts from its coverage criminal law, communications privacy law, and "intellectual property claims." In interpreting these exclusions, courts agree that Congress meant to exclude federal intellectual property claims, such as copyright and trademark, but they disagree whether state-law intellectual property claims (or claims that arguably could be classified as intellectual property claims, such as the right of publicity) are also exempted from the broad immunity protection Section 230 provides. Finally, Section 230 does not immunize the actual creator of content. The author of a defamatory statement, whether he is a blogger, commenter, or anything else, remains just as responsible for his online statements as he would be for his offline statements.

Online Activities Covered by Section 230

Courts have consistently held that exercising traditional editorial functions over user-submitted content, such as deciding whether to publish, remove, or edit material, is immunized under Section 230. As one moves farther away from these basic functions, immunity may still exist, but the analysis becomes more fact-specific. We analyze in detail the types of activites that are covered by Section 230 and those activities that fall outside its protections in the Online Activities Covered by Section 230 [11] and Online Activities Not Covered by Section 230 [12] pages of this legal guide. (We strongly advise that you review these pages if your activities extend beyond traditional editorial functions.)

Summary
Section 230 of the Communications Decency Act grants interactive online services of all types, including blogs, forums, and listservs, broad immunity

from tort liability so long as the information at issue is provided by a third party. Relatively few court decisions, however, have analyzed the scope of this immunity in the context of "mixed content" that is created jointly by the operator of the interactive service and a third party through significant editing of content or the shaping of content by submission forms and drop-downs.

So what are the practical things you can take away from this guide? Here are five:

1.   If you **passively host third-party content**, you will be fully protected under Section 230.

2.   If you **exercise traditional editorial functions** over user submitted content, such as deciding whether to publish, remove, or edit material, you will not lose your immunity unless your edits materially alter the meaning of the content.

3.   If you **pre-screen objectionable content** or correct, edit, or remove content, you will not lose your immunity.

4.   If you **encourage or pay third-parties to create or submit content**, you will not lose your immunity.

5.   If you use **drop-down forms or multiple-choice questionnaires**, you should be cautious of allowing users to submit information through these forms that might be deemed illegal.

To follow recent developments in the law concerning these immunity provisions, see our Section 230 summary page [13], where you will find background on Section 230, links to our legal guide materials, and feeds showing recent legal threats from our database [14], blog posts [15], and news.

- Online Activities Covered by Section 230 [11]
- Online Activities Not Covered by Section 230 [12]
- Publishing the Statements and Content of Others [4]up [4]Online Activities Covered by Section 230[11]
- United States
- Section 230
- Third-Party Content

Source URL (retrieved on *05/25/2011 - 5:55pm*): http://www.citmedialaw.
org/legal-guide/immunity-online-publishers-under-communications-
decency-act
Links:

[1] http://www.law.cornell.edu/uscode/html/uscode47/usc_
sec_47_00000230----000-.html
[2] http://www.citmedialaw.org/glossary/8/letteri#term218
[3] http://www.citmedialaw.org/glossary/8/letterl#term272
[4] http://www.citmedialaw.org/legal-guide/publishing-statements-and-
content-others
[5] http://www.citmedialaw.org/glossary/8/letterd#term212
[6] http://www.citmedialaw.org/glossary/8/lettera#term262
[7] http://www.citmedialaw.org/threats/cubby-v-compuserve
[8] http://www.citmedialaw.org/threats/stratton-oakmont-v-prodigy
[9] http://frwebgate.access.gpo.gov/cgi-bin/getdoc.cgi?dbname=104_
cong_public_laws&docid=f:publ104.104.pdf
[10] http://www.citmedialaw.org/threats/doe-v-myspace
[11] http://www.citmedialaw.org/legal-guide/online-activities-covered-
section-230
[12] http://www.citmedialaw.org/legal-guide/online-activities-not-
covered-section-230
[13] http://www.citmedialaw.org/section-230
[14] http://www.citmedialaw.org/database
[15] http://www.citmedialaw.org/blog

Appendix Three
The Digital Millennium
Copyright Act of 1998

Source: The Library of Congress

The Digital Millennium Copyright Act (DMCA) was signed into law by President Clinton on October 28, 1998. The legislation implements two 1996 World Intellectual Property Organization (WIPO) treaties: the WIPO Copyright Treaty and the WIPO Performances and Phonograms Treaty. The DMCA also addresses a number of other significant copyright-related issues.

H.R.2281

One Hundred Fifth Congress

of the

United States of America

AT THE SECOND SESSION

Begun and held at the City of Washington on Tuesday,
the twenty-seventh day of January, one thousand nine hundred and ninety-eight

An Act

To amend title 17, United States Code, to implement the World Intellectual

Property Organization Copyright Treaty and Performances and Phonograms Treaty, and for other purposes.

Be it enacted by the Senate and House of Representatives of the United States of America in Congress assembled,

7. SECTION 1. SHORT TITLE.

This Act may be cited as the 'Digital Millennium Copyright Act.'

8. SEC. 2. TABLE OF CONTENTS.

9. TITLE I—WIPO TREATIES IMPLEMENTATION

10. TITLE II—ONLINE COPYRIGHT INFRINGEMENT LIABILITY LIMITATION

11. TITLE III—COMPUTER MAINTENANCE OR REPAIR COPYRIGHT EXEMPTION

12. TITLE IV—MISCELLANEOUS PROVISIONS

Sec. 404. Exemption for libraries and archives.

Sec. 405. Scope of exclusive rights in sound recordings; ephemeral recordings.

Sec. 406. Assumption of contractual obligations related to transfers of rights in motion pictures.

Sec. 407. Effective date.

13. TITLE V—PROTECTION OF CERTAIN ORIGINAL DESIGNS

Sec. 501. Short title.

Sec. 502. Protection of certain original designs.

Sec. 503. Conforming amendments.

Sec. 504. Joint study of the effect of this title.

Sec. 505. Effective date.

1.   TITLE I—WIPO TREATIES IMPLEMENTATION

14. SEC. 101. SHORT TITLE.

This title may be cited as the 'WIPO Copyright and Performances and Phonograms Treaties Implementation Act of 1998'.

15. SEC. 102. TECHNICAL AMENDMENTS.

(a) DEFINITIONS- Section 101 of title 17, United States Code, is amended--

(1) by striking the definition of 'Berne Convention work';

(2) in the definition of 'The 'country of origin' of a Berne Convention work'--

(A) by striking 'The 'country of origin' of a Berne Convention work, for purposes of section 411, is the United States if' and inserting 'For purposes of section 411, a work is a 'United States work' only if';

(B) in paragraph (1)--

(i) in subparagraph (B) by striking 'nation or nations adhering to the Berne Convention' and inserting 'treaty party or parties';

(ii) in subparagraph (C) by striking 'does not adhere to the Berne Convention' and inserting 'is not a treaty party'; and

(iii) in subparagraph (D) by striking 'does not adhere to the Berne Convention' and inserting 'is not a treaty party'; and

(C) in the matter following paragraph (3) by striking 'For the purposes of section 411, the 'country of origin' of any other Berne Convention work is not the United States;

(3) by inserting after the definition of 'fixed' the following:

'The 'Geneva Phonograms Convention' is the Convention for the Protection of Producers of Phonograms Against Unauthorized Duplication of Their Phonograms, concluded at Geneva, Switzerland, on October 29, 1971.';

(4) by inserting after the definition of 'including' the following:

'An 'international agreement' is--

(1) the Universal Copyright Convention;

(2) the Geneva Phonograms Convention;

(3) the Berne Convention;

(4) the WTO Agreement;

(5) the WIPO Copyright Treaty;

(6) the WIPO Performances and Phonograms Treaty; and

(7) any other copyright treaty to which the United States is a party.';

(5) by inserting after the definition of 'transmit' the following:

A 'treaty party' is a country or intergovernmental organization other than the United States that is a party to an international agreement;

(6) by inserting after the definition of 'widow' the following:

'The 'WIPO Copyright Treaty' is the WIPO Copyright Treaty concluded at Geneva, Switzerland, on December 20, 1996.';

(7) by inserting after the definition of 'The 'WIPO Copyright Treaty' the following: 'The 'WIPO Performances and Phonograms Treaty' is the WIPO Performances and Phonograms Treaty concluded at Geneva, Switzerland, on December 20, 1996.'; and

(8) by inserting after the definition of 'work made for hire' the following:

'The terms 'WTO Agreement' and 'WTO member country' have the meanings given those terms in paragraphs (9) and (10), respectively, of section 2 of the Uruguay Round Agreements Act.'.

(b) SUBJECT MATTER OF COPYRIGHT; NATIONAL ORIGIN- Section 104 of title 17, United States Code, is amended--

(1) in subsection (b)--

(A) in paragraph (1) by striking 'foreign nation that is a party to a copyright treaty to which the United States is also a party' and inserting 'treaty party';

(B) in paragraph (2) by striking 'party to the Universal Copyright Convention' and inserting 'treaty party';

(C) by redesignating paragraph (5) as paragraph (6);

(D) by redesignating paragraph (3) as paragraph (5) and inserting it after paragraph (4);

(E) by inserting after paragraph (2) the following:

'(3) the work is a sound recording that was first fixed in a treaty party; or';

(F) in paragraph (4) by striking 'Berne Convention work' and inserting 'pictorial, graphic, or sculptural work that is incorporated in a building or other structure, or an architectural work that is embodied in a building and the building or structure is located in the United States or a treaty party'; and

(G) by inserting after paragraph (6), as so redesignated, the following:

'For purposes of paragraph (2), a work that is published in the United States or a treaty party within 30 days after publication in a foreign nation that is not a treaty party shall be considered to be first published in the United States or such treaty party, as the case may be.'; and

(2) by adding at the end the following new subsection:

'(d) EFFECT OF PHONOGRAMS TREATIES- Notwithstanding the provisions of subsection (b), no works other than sound recordings shall be eligible for protection under this title solely by virtue of the adherence of the United States to the Geneva Phonograms Convention or the WIPO Performances and Phonograms Treaty.'.

(c) COPYRIGHT IN RESTORED WORKS- Section 104A(h) of title 17, United States Code, is amended--

(1) in paragraph (1), by striking subparagraphs (A) and (B) and inserting the following:

(A) a nation adhering to the Berne Convention;

(B) a WTO member country;

(C) a nation adhering to the WIPO Copyright Treaty;

(D) a nation adhering to the WIPO Performances and Phonograms Treaty; or

(E) subject to a Presidential proclamation under subsection (g).';

(2) by amending paragraph (3) to read as follows:

(3) The term 'eligible country' means a nation, other than the United States, that--

(A) becomes a WTO member country after the date of the enactment of the Uruguay Round Agreements Act;

(B) on such date of enactment is, or after such date of enactment becomes, a nation adhering to the Berne Convention;

(C) adheres to the WIPO Copyright Treaty;

(D) adheres to the WIPO Performances and Phonograms Treaty; or

(E) after such date of enactment becomes subject to a proclamation under subsection (g).';

(3) in paragraph (6)--

(A) in subparagraph (C)(iii) by striking 'and' after the semicolon;

(B) at the end of subparagraph (D) by striking the period and inserting '; and'; and

(C) by adding after subparagraph (D) the following:

(E) if the source country for the work is an eligible country solely by virtue of its adherence to the WIPO Performances and Phonograms Treaty, is a sound recording.';

(4) in paragraph (8)(B)(i)--

(A) by inserting 'of which' before 'the majority'; and

(B) by striking 'of eligible countries'; and

(5) by striking paragraph (9).

(d) REGISTRATION AND INFRINGEMENT ACTIONS- Section 411(a) of title 17, United States Code, is amended in the first sentence--

(1) by striking 'actions for infringement of copyright in Berne Convention works whose country of origin is not the United States and'; and

(2) by inserting 'United States' after 'no action for infringement of the copyright in any'.

(e) STATUTE OF LIMITATIONS- Section 507(a) of title 17, United State Code, is amended by striking 'No' and inserting 'Except as expressly provided otherwise in this title, no'.

16. SEC. 103. COPYRIGHT PROTECTION SYSTEMS AND COPYRIGHT MANAGEMENT INFORMATION.

(a) IN GENERAL- Title 17, United States Code, is amended by adding at the end the following new chapter:

1. CHAPTER 12--COPYRIGHT PROTECTION AND MANAGEMENT SYSTEMS

Sec.

1201. Circumvention of copyright protection systems.

1202. Integrity of copyright management information.

1203. Civil remedies.

1204. Criminal offenses and penalties.

1205. Savings clause.

1. Sec. 1201. Circumvention of copyright protection systems

(a) VIOLATIONS REGARDING CIRCUMVENTION OF TECHNOLOGICAL MEASURES- (1)(A) No person shall circumvent a technological measure that effectively controls access to a work protected under this title. The prohibition contained in the preceding sentence shall take effect at the end of the 2-year period beginning on the date of the enactment of this chapter.

(b) The prohibition contained in subparagraph (A) shall not apply to persons who are users of a copyrighted work which is in a particular class of works, if such persons are, or are likely to be in the succeeding 3-year period, adversely affected by virtue of such prohibition in their ability to make noninfringing uses of that particular class of works under this title, as determined under subparagraph (C).

(c) During the 2-year period described in subparagraph (A), and during each succeeding 3-year period, the Librarian of Congress, upon the recommendation of the Register of Copyrights, who shall consult with the Assistant Secretary for Communications and Information of the Department of Commerce and report and comment on his or her views in making such recommendation, shall make the determination in a rulemaking proceeding on the record for purposes of subparagraph (B) of whether persons who are users of a copyrighted work are, or are likely to be in the succeeding 3-year period, adversely affected by the prohibition under subparagraph (A) in their ability to make noninfringing uses under this title of a particular class of copyrighted works. In conducting such rulemaking, the Librarian shall examine--

(i) the availability for use of copyrighted works;

(ii) the availability for use of works for nonprofit archival, preservation, and educational purposes;

(iii) the impact that the prohibition on the circumvention of technological measures applied to copyrighted works has on criticism, comment, news reporting, teaching, scholarship, or research;

(iv) the effect of circumvention of technological measures on the market for or value of copyrighted works; and

(v) such other factors as the Librarian considers appropriate.

(D) The Librarian shall publish any class of copyrighted works for which the Librarian has determined, pursuant to the rulemaking conducted under subparagraph (C), that noninfringing uses by persons who are users of a copyrighted work are, or are likely to be, adversely affected, and the prohibition contained in subparagraph (A) shall not apply to such users with respect to such class of works for the ensuing 3-year period.

(E) Neither the exception under subparagraph (B) from the applicability of the prohibition contained in subparagraph (A), nor any determination made in a rulemaking conducted under subparagraph (C), may be used as a defense in any action to enforce any provision of this title other than this paragraph.

(2) No person shall manufacture, import, offer to the public, provide, or otherwise traffic in any technology, product, service, device, component, or part thereof, that--

(A) is primarily designed or produced for the purpose of circumventing a technological measure that effectively controls access to a work protected under this title;

(B) has only limited commercially significant purpose or use other than to circumvent a technological measure that effectively controls access to a work protected under this title; or

(C) is marketed by that person or another acting in concert with that person with that person's knowledge for use in circumventing a technological measure that effectively controls access to a work protected under this title.

(3) As used in this subsection--

(A) to 'circumvent a technological measure' means to descramble a scrambled work, to decrypt an encrypted work, or otherwise to avoid, bypass, remove, deactivate, or impair a technological measure, without the authority of the copyright owner; and

(B) a technological measure 'effectively controls access to a work' if the measure, in the ordinary course of its operation, requires the application of information, or a process or a treatment, with the authority of the copyright owner, to gain access to the work.

(b) ADDITIONAL VIOLATIONS- (1) No person shall manufacture, import, offer to the public, provide, or otherwise traffic in any technology, product, service, device, component, or part thereof, that--

(A) is primarily designed or produced for the purpose of circumventing protection afforded by a technological measure that effectively protects a right of a copyright owner under this title in a work or a portion thereof;

(B) has only limited commercially significant purpose or use other than to circumvent protection afforded by a technological measure that effectively protects a right of a copyright owner under this title in a work or a portion thereof; or

(C) is marketed by that person or another acting in concert with that person with that person's knowledge for use in circumventing protection afforded by a technological measure that effectively protects a right of a copyright owner under this title in a work or a portion thereof.

(1) As used in this subsection--

(A) to 'circumvent protection afforded by a technological measure' means avoiding, bypassing, removing, deactivating, or otherwise impairing a technological measure; and

(B) a technological measure 'effectively protects a right of a copyright owner under this title' if the measure, in the ordinary course of its operation, prevents, restricts, or otherwise limits the exercise of a right of a copyright owner under this title.

(C) OTHER RIGHTS, ETC., NOT AFFECTED- (1) Nothing in this section shall affect rights, remedies, limitations, or defenses to copyright infringement, including fair use, under this title.

(2) Nothing in this section shall enlarge or diminish vicarious or contributory liability for copyright infringement in connection with any technology, product, service, device, component, or part thereof.

(3) Nothing in this section shall require that the design of, or design and selection of parts and components for, a consumer electronics, telecommunications, or computing product provide for a response to any particular technological measure, so long as such part or component, or the product in which such part or component is integrated, does not otherwise fall within the prohibitions of subsection (a)(2) or (b)(1).

(4) Nothing in this section shall enlarge or diminish any rights of free speech or the press for activities using consumer electronics, telecommunications, or computing products.

(d) EXEMPTION FOR NONPROFIT LIBRARIES, ARCHIVES, AND EDUCATIONAL INSTITUTIONS- (1) A nonprofit library, archives, or educational institution which gains access to a commercially exploited copyrighted work solely in order to make a good faith determination of whether to acquire a copy of that work for the sole purpose of engaging in conduct permitted under this title shall not be in violation of subsection (a)(1)(A). A copy of a work to which access has been gained under this paragraph--

(A) may not be retained longer than necessary to make such good faith determination; and

(B) may not be used for any other purpose.

(2) The exemption made available under paragraph (1) shall only apply with respect to a work when an identical copy of that work is not reasonably available in another form.

(3) A nonprofit library, archives, or educational institution that willfully for the purpose of commercial advantage or financial gain violates paragraph (1)--

(A) shall, for the first offense, be subject to the civil remedies under section 1203; and

(B) shall, for repeated or subsequent offenses, in addition to the civil remedies under section 1203, forfeit the exemption provided under paragraph (1).

(4) This subsection may not be used as a defense to a claim under subsection (a)(2) or (b), nor may this subsection permit a nonprofit library, archives, or educational institution to manufacture, import, offer to the public, provide, or otherwise traffic in any technology, product, service, component, or part thereof, which circumvents a technological measure.

(5) In order for a library or archives to qualify for the exemption under this subsection, the collections of that library or archives shall be--

(A) open to the public; or

(B) available not only to researchers affiliated with the library or archives or with the institution of which it is a part, but also to other persons doing research in a specialized field.

(e) LAW ENFORCEMENT, INTELLIGENCE, AND OTHER GOVERNMENT ACTIVITIES- This section does not prohibit any lawfully authorized investigative, protective, information security, or intelligence activity of an officer, agent, or employee of the United States, a State, or a political subdivision of a State, or a person acting pursuant to a contract with the United States, a State, or a political subdivision of a State. For purposes of this subsection, the term 'information security' means activities carried out in order to identify and address the vulnerabilities of a government computer, computer system, or computer network.

(f) REVERSE ENGINEERING- (1) Notwithstanding the provisions of subsection (a)(1)(A), a person who has lawfully obtained the right to use a copy of a computer program may circumvent a technological measure that effectively controls access to a particular portion of that program for the sole purpose of identifying and analyzing those elements of the program that are necessary to achieve interoperability of an independently created computer program with other programs, and that have not previously been readily available to the person engaging in the circumvention, to the extent any such acts of identification and analysis do not constitute infringement under this title.

(2) Notwithstanding the provisions of subsections (a)(2) and (b), a person may develop and employ technological means to circumvent a technological measure, or to circumvent protection afforded by a technological measure, in order to enable the identification and analysis under paragraph (1), or for the purpose of enabling interoperability of an independently created computer program with other programs, if such means are necessary to achieve such interoperability, to the extent that doing so does not constitute infringement under this title.

(3) The information acquired through the acts permitted under paragraph (1), and the means permitted under paragraph (2), may be made available to others if the person referred to in paragraph (1) or (2), as the case may be, provides such information or means solely for the purpose of enabling interoperability of an independently created computer program with other programs, and to the extent that doing so does not constitute infringement under this title or violate applicable law other than this section.

(4) For purposes of this subsection, the term 'interoperability' means the ability of computer programs to exchange information, and of such programs mutually to use the information which has been exchanged.

(g) ENCRYPTION RESEARCH-

(1) DEFINITIONS—For purposes of this subsection:

(A) the term 'encryption research' means activities necessary to identify and analyze flaws and vulnerabilities of encryption technologies applied to copyrighted works, if these activities are conducted to advance the state of knowledge in the field of encryption technology or to assist in the development of encryption products; and

(B) the term 'encryption technology' means the scrambling and descrambling of information using mathematical formulas or algorithms.

(2) PERMISSIBLE ACTS OF ENCRYPTION RESEARCH:

Notwithstanding the provisions of subsection (a)(1)(A), it is not a violation of that subsection for a person to circumvent a technological measure as applied to a copy, phonorecord, performance, or display of a published work in the course of an act of good faith encryption research if:

(A) the person lawfully obtained the encrypted copy, phonorecord, performance, or display of the published work;

(B) such act is necessary to conduct such encryption research;

(C) the person made a good faith effort to obtain authorization before the circumvention; and

(D) such act does not constitute infringement under this title or a violation of applicable law other than this section, including section 1030 of title 18 and those provisions of title 18 amended by the Computer Fraud and Abuse Act of 1986.

(3) FACTORS IN DETERMINING EXEMPTION—In determining whether a person qualifies for the exemption under paragraph (2), the factors to be considered shall include:

(A) whether the information derived from the encryption research was disseminated, and if so, whether it was disseminated in a manner reasonably calculated to advance the state of knowledge or development of encryption technology, versus whether it was disseminated in a manner that facilitates infringement under this title or a violation of applicable law other than this section, including a violation of privacy or breach of security;

(B) whether the person is engaged in a legitimate course of study, is employed, or is appropriately trained or experienced, in the field of encryption technology; and

(C) whether the person provides the copyright owner of the work to which the technological measure is applied with notice of the findings and documentation of the research, and the time when such notice is provided.

(4) USE OF TECHNOLOGICAL MEANS FOR RESEARCH ACTIVITIES:

Notwithstanding the provisions of subsection (a)(2), it is not a violation of that subsection for a person to:

(A) develop and employ technological means to circumvent a technological measure for the sole purpose of that person performing the acts of good faith encryption research described in paragraph (2); and

(B) provide the technological means to another person with whom he or she is working collaboratively for the purpose of conducting the acts of good faith encryption research described in paragraph (2) or for the purpose of having that other person verify his or her acts of good faith encryption research described in paragraph (2).

(5) REPORT TO CONGRESS—Not later than 1 year after the date of the enactment of this chapter, the Register of Copyrights and the Assistant Secretary for Communications and Information of the Department of Commerce shall jointly report to the Congress on the effect this subsection has had on:

(A) encryption research and the development of encryption technology;

(B) the adequacy and effectiveness of technological measures designed to protect copyrighted works; and

(C) protection of copyright owners against the unauthorized access to their encrypted copyrighted works.

The report shall include legislative recommendations, if any.

(h) EXCEPTIONS REGARDING MINORS- In applying subsection (a) to a component or part, the court may consider the necessity for its intended and actual incorporation in a technology, product, service, or device, which--

(1) does not itself violate the provisions of this title; and

(2) has the sole purpose to prevent the access of minors to material on the Internet.

(i) PROTECTION OF PERSONALLY IDENTIFYING INFORMATION-

(1) CIRCUMVENTION PERMITTED- Notwithstanding the provisions of subsection (a)(1)(A), it is not a violation of that subsection for a person to circumvent a technological measure that effectively controls access to a work protected under this title, if:

(A) the technological measure, or the work it protects, contains the capability of collecting or disseminating personally identifying information reflecting the online activities of a natural person who seeks to gain access to the work protected;

(B) in the normal course of its operation, the technological measure, or the work it protects, collects or disseminates personally identifying information about the person who seeks to gain access to the work protected, without providing conspicuous notice of such collection or dissemination to such person, and without providing such person with the capability to prevent or restrict such collection or dissemination;

(C) the act of circumvention has the sole effect of identifying and disabling the capability described in subparagraph (A), and has no other effect on the ability of any person to gain access to any work; and

(D) the act of circumvention is carried out solely for the purpose of preventing the collection or dissemination of personally identifying information about a natural person who seeks to gain access to the work protected, and is not in violation of any other law.

(2) INAPPLICABILITY TO CERTAIN TECHNOLOGICAL MEASURES- This subsection does not apply to a technological measure, or a work it protects, that does not collect or disseminate personally identifying information and that is disclosed to a user as not having or using such capability

(j) SECURITY TESTING

(1) DEFINITION: For purposes of this subsection, the term 'security testing' means accessing a computer, computer system, or computer network, solely for the purpose of good faith testing, investigating, or correcting, a security flaw or vulnerability, with the authorization of the owner or operator of such computer, computer system, or computer network.

(2) PERMISSIBLE ACTS OF SECURITY TESTING: Notwithstanding the provisions of subsection (a)(1)(A), it is not a violation of that subsection for a person to engage in an act of security testing, if such act does not constitute infringement under this title or a violation of applicable law other than this section, including section 1030 of title 18 and those provisions of title 18 amended by the Computer Fraud and Abuse Act of 1986.

(3) FACTORS IN DETERMINING EXEMPTION: In determining whether a person qualifies for the exemption under paragraph (2), the factors to be considered shall include:

(A) whether the information derived from the security testing was used solely to promote the security of the owner or operator of such computer, computer system or computer network, or shared directly with the developer of such computer, computer system, or computer network; and

(B) whether the information derived from the security testing was used or maintained in a manner that does not facilitate infringement under this title or a

149

violation of applicable law other than this section, including a violation of privacy or breach of security.

(4) USE OF TECHNOLOGICAL MEANS FOR SECURITY TESTING— Notwithstanding the provisions of subsection (a)(2), it is not a violation of that subsection for a person to develop, produce, distribute or employ technological means for the sole purpose of performing the acts of security testing described in subsection (2), provided such technological means does not otherwise violate section (a)(2).

(k) CERTAIN ANALOG DEVICES AND CERTAIN TECHNOLOGICAL MEASURES-

(1) CERTAIN ANALOG DEVICES-

(A) Effective 18 months after the date of the enactment of this chapter, no person shall manufacture, import, offer to the public, provide or otherwise traffic in any:

(i) VHS format analog video cassette recorder unless such recorder conforms to the automatic gain control copy control technology;

(ii) 8mm format analog video cassette camcorder unless such camcorder conforms to the automatic gain control technology;

(iii) Beta format analog video cassette recorder, unless such recorder conforms to the automatic gain control copy control technology, except that this requirement shall not apply until there are 1,000 Beta format analog video cassette recorders sold in the United States in any one calendar year after the date of the enactment of this chapter;

(iv) 8mm format analog video cassette recorder that is not an analog video cassette camcorder, unless such recorder conforms to the automatic gain control copy control technology, except that this requirement shall not apply until there are 20,000 such recorders sold in the United States in any one calendar year after the date of the enactment of this chapter; or

(v) analog video cassette recorder that records using an NTSC format video input and that is not otherwise covered under clauses (i) through (iv), unless such device conforms to the automatic gain control copy control technology.

(B) Effective on the date of the enactment of this chapter, no person shall manufacture, import, offer to the public, provide or otherwise traffic in:

(i) any VHS format analog video cassette recorder or any 8mm format analog video cassette recorder if the design of the model of such recorder has been modified after such date of enactment so that a model of recorder that previously conformed to the automatic gain control copy control technology no longer conforms to such technology; or

(ii) any VHS format analog video cassette recorder, or any 8mm format analog video cassette recorder that is not an 8mm analog video cassette camcorder, if the design of the model of such recorder has been modified after such date of enactment so that a model of recorder that previously conformed to the four-line colorstripe copy control technology no longer conforms to such technology.

Manufacturers that have not previously manufactured or sold a VHS format analog video cassette recorder, or an 8mm format analog cassette recorder, shall be required to conform to the four-line colorstripe copy control technology in the initial model of any such recorder manufactured after the date of the enactment of this chapter, and thereafter to continue conforming to the four-line colorstripe copy control technology. For purposes of this subparagraph, an analog video cassette recorder 'conforms to' the four-line colorstripe copy control technology if it records a signal that, when played back by the playback function of that recorder in the normal viewing mode, exhibits, on a reference display device, a display containing distracting visible lines through portions of the viewable picture.

(2) CERTAIN ENCODING RESTRICTIONS—No person shall apply the automatic gain control copy control technology or colorstripe copy control technology to prevent or limit consumer copying except such copying:

(A) of a single transmission, or specified group of transmissions, of live events or of audiovisual works for which a member of the public has exercised choice in selecting the transmissions, including the content of the transmissions or the time of receipt of such transmissions, or both, and as to which such member is charged a separate fee for each such transmission or specified group of transmissions;

(B) from a copy of a transmission of a live event or an audiovisual work if such transmission is provided by a channel or service where payment is made by a member of the public for such channel or service in the form of a subscription fee that entitles the member of the public to receive all of the programming contained in such channel or service;

(C) from a physical medium containing one or more prerecorded audiovisual works; or

(D) from a copy of a transmission described in subparagraph (A) or from a copy made from a physical medium described in subparagraph (C). In the event that a transmission meets both the conditions set forth in subparagraph (A) and those set forth in subparagraph (B), the transmission shall be treated as a transmission described in subparagraph (A).

(3) INAPPLICABILITY—This subsection shall not:

(A) require any analog video cassette camcorder to conform to the automatic gain control copy control technology with respect to any video signal received through a camera lens;

(B) apply to the manufacture, importation, offer for sale, provision of, or other trafficking in, any professional analog video cassette recorder; or

(C) apply to the offer for sale or provision of, or other trafficking in, any previously owned analog video cassette recorder, if such recorder was legally manufactured and sold when new and not subsequently modified in violation of paragraph (1)(B).

(4) DEFINITIONS—For purposes of this subsection:

(A) An 'analog video cassette recorder' means a device that records, or a device that includes a function that records, on electromagnetic tape in an analog format the electronic impulses produced by the video and audio portions of a television program, motion picture, or other form of audiovisual work.

(B) An 'analog video cassette camcorder' means an analog video cassette recorder that contains a recording function that operates through a camera lens and through a video input that may be connected with a television or other video playback device.

(C) An analog video cassette recorder 'conforms' to the automatic gain control copy control technology if it:

(i) detects one or more of the elements of such technology and does not record the motion picture or transmission protected by such technology; or

(ii) records a signal that, when played back, exhibits a meaningfully distorted or degraded display.

(D) The term 'professional analog video cassette recorder' means an analog video cassette recorder that is designed, manufactured, marketed, and intended for use by a person who regularly employs such a device for a lawful business or industrial use, including making, performing, displaying, distributing, or transmitting copies of motion pictures on a commercial scale.

(E) The terms 'VHS format', '8mm format', 'Beta format', 'automatic gain control copy control technology', 'colorstripe copy control technology', 'four-line version of the colorstripe copy control technology', and 'NTSC' have the meanings that are commonly understood in the consumer electronics and motion picture industries as of the date of the enactment of this chapter.

(5) VIOLATIONS—Any violation of paragraph (1) of this subsection shall be treated as a violation of subsection (b)(1) of this section. Any violation of paragraph

(2) of this subsection shall be deemed an 'act of circumvention' for the purposes of section 1203(c)(3)(A) of this chapter.

2.   **Sec. 1202. Integrity of copyright management information**

(a) FALSE COPYRIGHT MANAGEMENT INFORMATION- No person shall knowingly and with the intent to induce, enable, facilitate, or conceal infringement:

(1) provide copyright management information that is false, or

(2) distribute or import for distribution copyright management information that is false.

(b) REMOVAL OR ALTERATION OF COPYRIGHT MANAGEMENT INFORMATION—No person shall, without the authority of the copyright owner or the law:

(1) intentionally remove or alter any copyright management information,

(2) distribute or import for distribution copyright management information knowing that the copyright management information has been removed or altered without authority of the copyright owner or the law, or

(3) distribute, import for distribution, or publicly perform works, copies of works, or phonorecords, knowing that copyright management information has been removed or altered without authority of the copyright owner or the law, knowing, or, with respect to civil remedies under section 1203, having reasonable grounds to know, that it will induce, enable, facilitate, or conceal an infringement of any right under this title.

(c) DEFINITION—As used in this section, the term 'copyright management information' means any of the following information conveyed in connection with copies or phonorecords of a work or performances or displays of a work, including in digital form, except that such term does not include any personally identifying information about a user of a work or of a copy, phonorecord, performance, or display of a work:

(1) The title and other information identifying the work, including the information set forth on a notice of copyright.

(2) The name of, and other identifying information about, the author of a work.

(3) The name of, and other identifying information about, the copyright owner of the work, including the information set forth in a notice of copyright.

(4) With the exception of public performances of works by radio and television broadcast stations, the name of, and other identifying information about, a performer whose performance is fixed in a work other than an audiovisual work.

(5) With the exception of public performances of works by radio and television broadcast stations, in the case of an audiovisual work, the name of, and other identifying information about, a writer, performer, or director who is credited in the audiovisual work.

(6) Terms and conditions for use of the work.

(7) Identifying numbers or symbols referring to such information or links to such information.

(8) Such other information as the Register of Copyrights may prescribe by regulation, except that the Register of Copyrights may not require the provision of any information concerning the user of a copyrighted work.

(d) LAW ENFORCEMENT, INTELLIGENCE, AND OTHER GOVERNMENT ACTIVITIES- This section does not prohibit any lawfully authorized investigative, protective, information security, or intelligence activity of an officer, agent, or employee of the United States, a State, or a political subdivision of a State, or a person acting pursuant to a contract with the United States, a State, or a political subdivision of a State. For purposes of this subsection, the term 'information security' means activities carried out in order to identify and address the vulnerabilities of a government computer, computer system, or computer network.

(e) LIMITATIONS ON LIABILITY:

(1) ANALOG TRANSMISSIONS- In the case of an analog transmission, a person who is making transmissions in its capacity as a broadcast station, or as a cable system, or someone who provides programming to such station or system, shall not be liable for a violation of subsection (b) if:

(A) avoiding the activity that constitutes such violation is not technically feasible or would create an undue financial hardship on such person; and

(B) such person did not intend, by engaging in such activity, to induce, enable, facilitate, or conceal infringement of a right under this title.

(2) DIGITAL TRANSMISSIONS-

(A) If a digital transmission standard for the placement of copyright management information for a category of works is set in a voluntary, consensus standard-setting process involving a representative cross-section of broadcast stations or cable systems and copyright owners of a category of works that are intended for public performance by such stations or systems, a person identified in paragraph (1) shall not be liable for a violation of subsection (b) with respect to the particular copyright management information addressed by such standard if--

(i) the placement of such information by someone other than such person is not in accordance with such standard; and

(ii) the activity that constitutes such violation is not intended to induce, enable, facilitate, or conceal infringement of a right under this title.

(B) Until a digital transmission standard has been set pursuant to subparagraph (A) with respect to the placement of copyright management information for a category or works, a person identified in paragraph (1) shall not be liable for a violation of subsection (b) with respect to such copyright management information, if the activity that constitutes such violation is not intended to induce, enable, facilitate, or conceal infringement of a right under this title, and if--

(i) the transmission of such information by such person would result in a perceptible visual or aural degradation of the digital signal; or

(ii) the transmission of such information by such person would conflict with:

(I) an applicable government regulation relating to transmission of information in a digital signal;

(II) an applicable industry-wide standard relating to the transmission of information in a digital signal that was adopted by a voluntary consensus standards body prior to the effective date of this chapter; or

(III) an applicable industry-wide standard relating to the transmission of information in a digital signal that was adopted in a voluntary, consensus standards-setting process open to participation by a representative cross-section of broadcast stations or cable systems and copyright owners of a category of works that are intended for public performance by such stations or systems.

(3) DEFINITIONS—As used in this subsection:

(A) the term 'broadcast station' has the meaning given that term in section 3 of the Communications Act of 1934 (47 U.S.C. 153); and

(B) the term 'cable system' has the meaning given that term in section 602 of the Communications Act of 1934 (47 U.S.C. 522).

3. Sec. 1203. Civil remedies

(a) CIVIL ACTIONS: Any person injured by a violation of section 1201 or 1202 may bring a civil action in an appropriate United States district court for such violation.

(b) POWERS OF THE COURT—In an action brought under subsection (a), the court:

(1) may grant temporary and permanent injunctions on such terms as it deems reasonable to prevent or restrain a violation, but in no event shall impose a prior restraint on free speech or the press protected under the 1st amendment to the Constitution;

(2) at any time while an action is pending, may order the impounding, on such terms as it deems reasonable, of any device or product that is in the custody or control of the alleged violator and that the court has reasonable cause to believe was involved in a violation;

(3) may award damages under subsection (c);

(4) in its discretion may allow the recovery of costs by or against any party other than the United States or an officer thereof;

(5) in its discretion may award reasonable attorney's fees to the prevailing party; and

(6) may, as part of a final judgment or decree finding a violation, order the remedial modification or the destruction of any device or product involved in the violation that is in the custody or control of the violator or has been impounded under paragraph (2).

(c) AWARD OF DAMAGES:

(1) IN GENERAL—Except as otherwise provided in this title, a person committing a violation of section 1201 or 1202 is liable for either:

(A) the actual damages and any additional profits of the violator, as provided in paragraph (2), or

(B) statutory damages, as provided in paragraph (3).

(2) ACTUAL DAMAGES- The court shall award to the complaining party the actual damages suffered by the party as a result of the violation, and any profits of the violator that are attributable to the violation and are not taken into account in computing the actual damages, if the complaining party elects such damages at any time before final judgment is entered.

(3) STATUTORY DAMAGES- (A) At any time before final judgment is entered, a complaining party may elect to recover an award of statutory damages for each violation of section 1201 in the sum of not less than $200 or more than $2,500 per act of circumvention, device, product, component, offer, or performance of service, as the court considers just. At any time before final judgment is entered, a complaining party may elect to recover an award of statutory damages for each violation of section 1202 in the sum of not less than $2,500 or more than $25,000.

(4) REPEATED VIOLATIONS: In any case in which the injured party sustains the burden of proving, and the court finds, that a person has violated section 1201 or 1202 within 3 years after a final judgment was entered against the person for another such violation, the court may increase the award of damages up to triple the amount that would otherwise be awarded, as the court considers just.

(5) Innocent violations:

(A) IN GENERAL—The court in its discretion may reduce or remit the total award of damages in any case in which the violator sustains the burden of proving, and the court finds, that the violator was not aware and had no reason to believe that its acts constituted a violation.

(B) NONPROFIT LIBRARY, ARCHIVES, OR EDUCATIONAL INSTITUTIONS—In the case of a nonprofit library, archives, or educational institution, the court shall remit damages in any case in which the library, archives, or educational institution sustains the burden of proving, and the court finds, that the library, archives, or educational institution was not aware and had no reason to believe that its acts constituted a violation.

4. Sec. 1204. Criminal offenses and penalties

(a) IN GENERAL—Any person who violates section 1201 or 1202 willfully and for purposes of commercial advantage or private financial gain:

(1) shall be fined not more than $500,000 or imprisoned for not more than 5 years, or both, for the first offense; and

(2) shall be fined not more than $1,000,000 or imprisoned for not more than 10 years, or both, for any subsequent offense.

(b) LIMITATION FOR NONPROFIT LIBRARY, ARCHIVES, OR EDUCATIONAL INSTITUTION—Subsection (a) shall not apply to a nonprofit library, archives, or educational institution.

(c) STATUTE OF LIMITATIONS—No criminal proceeding shall be brought under this section unless such proceeding is commenced within 5 years after the cause of action arose.

5. Sec. 1205. Savings clause

Nothing in this chapter abrogates, diminishes, or weakens the provisions of, nor provides any defense or element of mitigation in a criminal prosecution or civil action under, any Federal or State law that prevents the violation of the privacy of an individual in connection with the individual's use of the Internet.'

(b) CONFORMING AMENDMENT—The table of chapters for title 17, United States Code, is amended by adding after the item relating to chapter 11 the following:

1201.SEC. 104. EVALUATION OF IMPACT OF COPYRIGHT LAW AND AMENDMENTS ON ELECTRONIC COMMERCE AND TECHNOLOGICAL DEVELOPMENT.

(a) EVALUATION BY THE REGISTER OF COPYRIGHTS AND THE ASSISTANT SECRETARY FOR COMMUNICATIONS AND INFORMATION— The Register of Copyrights and the Assistant Secretary for Communications and Information of the Department of Commerce shall jointly evaluate:

(1) the effects of the amendments made by this title and the development of electronic commerce and associated technology on the operation of sections 109 and 117 of title 17, United States Code; and

(2) the relationship between existing and emergent technology and the operation of sections 109 and 117 of title 17, United States Code.

(b) REPORT TO CONGRESS—The Register of Copyrights and the Assistant Secretary for Communications and Information of the Department of Commerce shall, not later than 24 months after the date of the enactment of this Act, submit to the Congress a joint report on the evaluation conducted under subsection (a), including any legislative recommendations the Register and the Assistant Secretary may have.

1. SEC. 105. EFFECTIVE DATE.

(a) IN GENERAL—Except as otherwise provided in this title, this title and the amendments made by this title shall take effect on the date of the enactment of this Act.

(b) AMENDMENTS RELATING TO CERTAIN INTERNATIONAL AGREEMENTS—(1) The following shall take effect upon the entry into force of the WIPO Copyright Treaty with respect to the United States:

(A) Paragraph (5) of the definition of 'international agreement' contained in section 101 of title 17, United States Code, as amended by section 102(a)(4) of this Act.

(B) The amendment made by section 102(a)(6) of this Act.

(C) Subparagraph (C) of section 104A(h)(1) of title 17, United States Code, as amended by section 102(c)(1) of this Act.

(D) Subparagraph (C) of section 104A(h)(3) of title 17, United States Code, as amended by section 102(c)(2) of this Act.

(2) The following shall take effect upon the entry into force of the WIPO Performances and Phonograms Treaty with respect to the United States:

(A) Paragraph (6) of the definition of 'international agreement' contained in section 101 of title 17, United States Code, as amended by section 102(a)(4) of this Act.

(B) The amendment made by section 102(a)(7) of this Act.

(C) The amendment made by section 102(b)(2) of this Act.

(D) Subparagraph (D) of section 104A(h)(1) of title 17, United States Code, as amended by section 102(c)(1) of this Act.

(E) Subparagraph (D) of section 104A(h)(3) of title 17, United States Code, as amended by section 102(c)(2) of this Act.

(F) The amendments made by section 102(c)(3) of this Act.

1. **TITLE II--ONLINE COPYRIGHT INFRINGEMENT LIABILITY LIMITATION**

2. **SEC. 201. SHORT TITLE.**

This title may be cited as the 'Online Copyright Infringement Liability Limitation Act.'

3. **SEC. 202. LIMITATIONS ON LIABILITY FOR COPYRIGHT INFRINGEMENT.**

(a) IN GENERAL—Chapter 5 of title 17, United States Code, is amended by adding after section 511 the following new section:

1. **Sec. 512. Limitations on liability relating to material online**

(a) TRANSITORY DIGITAL NETWORK COMMUNICATIONS—A service provider shall not be liable for monetary relief, or, except as provided in subsection (j), for injunctive or other equitable relief, for infringement of copyright by reason of the provider's transmitting, routing, or providing connections for, material through a system or network controlled or operated by or for the service provider, or by reason of the intermediate and transient storage of that material in the course of such transmitting, routing, or providing connections, if:

(1) the transmission of the material was initiated by or at the direction of a person other than the service provider;

(2) the transmission, routing, provision of connections, or storage is carried out through an automatic technical process without selection of the material by the service provider;

(3) the service provider does not select the recipients of the material except as an automatic response to the request of another person;

(4) no copy of the material made by the service provider in the course of such intermediate or transient storage is maintained on the system or network in a manner ordinarily accessible to anyone other than anticipated recipients, and no such copy

is maintained on the system or network in a manner ordinarily accessible to such anticipated recipients for a longer period than is reasonably necessary for the transmission, routing, or provision of connections; and

(5) the material is transmitted through the system or network without modification of its content.

(b) SYSTEM CACHING:

(1) LIMITATION ON LIABILITY—A service provider shall not be liable for monetary relief, or, except as provided in subsection (j), for injunctive or other equitable relief, for infringement of copyright by reason of the intermediate and temporary storage of material on a system or network controlled or operated by or for the service provider in a case in which:

(A) the material is made available online by a person other than the service provider;

(B) the material is transmitted from the person described in subparagraph (A) through the system or network to a person other than the person described in subparagraph (A) at the direction of that other person; and

(C) the storage is carried out through an automatic technical process for the purpose of making the material available to users of the system or network who, after the material is transmitted as described in subparagraph (B), request access to the material from the person described in subparagraph (A), if the conditions set forth in paragraph (2) are met.

(2) CONDITIONS—The conditions referred to in paragraph (1) are that:

(A) the material described in paragraph (1) is transmitted to the subsequent users described in paragraph (1)(C) without modification to its content from the manner in which the material was transmitted from the person described in paragraph (1)(A);

(B) the service provider described in paragraph (1) complies with rules concerning the refreshing, reloading, or other updating of the material when specified by the person making the material available online in accordance with a generally accepted industry standard data communications protocol for the system or network through which that person makes the material available, except that this subparagraph applies only if those rules are not used by the person described in paragraph (1)(A) to prevent or unreasonably impair the intermediate storage to which this subsection applies;

(C) the service provider does not interfere with the ability of technology associated with the material to return to the person described in paragraph (1)(A) the information that would have been available to that person if the material had been obtained by the subsequent users described in paragraph (1)(C) directly from that person, except that this subparagraph applies only if that technology:

(i) does not significantly interfere with the performance of the provider's system or network or with the intermediate storage of the material;

(ii) is consistent with generally accepted industry standard communications protocols; and

(iii) does not extract information from the provider's system or network other than the information that would have been available to the person described in paragraph (1)(A) if the subsequent users had gained access to the material directly from that person;

(D) if the person described in paragraph (1)(A) has in effect a condition that a person must meet prior to having access to the material, such as a condition based on payment of a fee or provision of a password or other information, the service provider permits access to the stored material in significant part only to users of its system or network that have met those conditions and only in accordance with those conditions; and

(E) if the person described in paragraph (1)(A) makes that material available online without the authorization of the copyright owner of the material, the service provider responds expeditiously to remove, or disable access to, the material that is claimed to be infringing upon notification of claimed infringement as described in subsection (c)(3), except that this subparagraph applies only if:

(i) the material has previously been removed from the originating site or access to it has been disabled, or a court has ordered that the material be removed from the originating site or that access to the material on the originating site be disabled; and

(ii) the party giving the notification includes in the notification a statement confirming that the material has been removed from the originating site or access to it has been disabled or that a court has ordered that the material be removed from the originating site or that access to the material on the originating site be disabled.

(c) INFORMATION RESIDING ON SYSTEMS OR NETWORKS AT DIRECTION OF USERS:

(1) IN GENERAL—A service provider shall not be liable for monetary relief, or, except as provided in subsection (j), for injunctive or other equitable relief, for infringement of copyright by reason of the storage at the direction of a user of material that resides on a system or network controlled or operated by or for the service provider, if the service provider:

(A)(i) does not have actual knowledge that the material or an activity using the material on the system or network is infringing;

(ii) in the absence of such actual knowledge, is not aware of facts or circumstances from which infringing activity is apparent; or

(iii) upon obtaining such knowledge or awareness, acts expeditiously to remove, or disable access to, the material;

(B) does not receive a financial benefit directly attributable to the infringing activity, in a case in which the service provider has the right and ability to control such activity; and

(C) upon notification of claimed infringement as described in paragraph (3), responds expeditiously to remove, or disable access to, the material that is claimed to be infringing or to be the subject of infringing activity.

(2) DESIGNATED AGENT—The limitations on liability established in this subsection apply to a service provider only if the service provider has designated an agent to receive notifications of claimed infringement described in paragraph (3), by making available through its service, including on its website in a location accessible to the public, and by providing to the Copyright Office, substantially the following information:

(A) the name, address, phone number, and electronic mail address of the agent.

(B) other contact information which the Register of Copyrights may deem appropriate.

The Register of Copyrights shall maintain a current directory of agents available to the public for inspection, including through the Internet, in both electronic and hard copy formats, and may require payment of a fee by service providers to cover the costs of maintaining the directory.

(3) ELEMENTS OF NOTIFICATION:

(A) To be effective under this subsection, a notification of claimed infringement must be a written communication provided to the designated agent of a service provider that includes substantially the following:

(i) A physical or electronic signature of a person authorized to act on behalf of the owner of an exclusive right that is allegedly infringed.

(ii) Identification of the copyrighted work claimed to have been infringed, or, if multiple copyrighted works at a single online site are covered by a single notification, a representative list of such works at that site.

(iii) Identification of the material that is claimed to be infringing or to be the subject of infringing activity and that is to be removed or access to which is to be disabled, and information reasonably sufficient to permit the service provider to locate the material.

(iv) Information reasonably sufficient to permit the service provider to contact the complaining party, such as an address, telephone number, and, if available, an electronic mail address at which the complaining party may be contacted.

(v) A statement that the complaining party has a good faith belief that use of the material in the manner complained of is not authorized by the copyright owner, its agent, or the law.

(vi) A statement that the information in the notification is accurate, and under penalty of perjury, that the complaining party is authorized to act on behalf of the owner of an exclusive right that is allegedly infringed.

(B)(i) Subject to clause (ii), a notification from a copyright owner or from a person authorized to act on behalf of the copyright owner that fails to comply substantially with the provisions of subparagraph (A) shall not be considered under paragraph (1)(A) in determining whether a service provider has actual knowledge or is aware of facts or circumstances from which infringing activity is apparent.

(ii) In a case in which the notification that is provided to the service provider's designated agent fails to comply substantially with all the provisions of subparagraph (A) but substantially complies with clauses (ii), (iii), and (iv) of subparagraph (A), clause (i) of this subparagraph applies only if the service provider promptly attempts to contact the person making the notification or takes other reasonable steps to assist in the receipt of notification that substantially complies with all the provisions of subparagraph (A).

(d) INFORMATION LOCATION TOOLS—A service provider shall not be liable for monetary relief, or, except as provided in subsection (j), for injunctive or other equitable relief, for infringement of copyright by reason of the provider referring or linking users to an online location containing infringing material or infringing activity, by using information location tools, including a directory, index, reference, pointer, or hypertext link, if the service provider:

(1)(A) does not have actual knowledge that the material or activity is infringing;

(B) in the absence of such actual knowledge, is not aware of facts or circumstances from which infringing activity is apparent; or

(C) upon obtaining such knowledge or awareness, acts expeditiously to remove, or disable access to, the material;

(2) does not receive a financial benefit directly attributable to the infringing activity, in a case in which the service provider has the right and ability to control such activity; and

(3) upon notification of claimed infringement as described in subsection (c)(3), responds expeditiously to remove, or disable access to, the material that is claimed to be infringing or to be the subject of infringing activity, except that, for purposes of this paragraph, the information described in subsection (c)(3)(A)(iii) shall be

identification of the reference or link, to material or activity claimed to be infringing, that is to be removed or access to which is to be disabled, and information reasonably sufficient to permit the service provider to locate that reference or link.

(e) LIMITATION ON LIABILITY OF NONPROFIT EDUCATIONAL INSTITUTIONS—(1) When a public or other nonprofit institution of higher education is a service provider, and when a faculty member or graduate student who is an employee of such institution is performing a teaching or research function, for the purposes of subsections (a) and (b) such faculty member or graduate student shall be considered to be a person other than the institution, and for the purposes of subsections (c) and (d) such faculty member's or graduate student's knowledge or awareness of his or her infringing activities shall not be attributed to the institution, if:

(A) such faculty member's or graduate student's infringing activities do not involve the provision of online access to instructional materials that are or were required or recommended, within the preceding 3-year period, for a course taught at the institution by such faculty member or graduate student;

(B) the institution has not, within the preceding 3-year period, received more than two notifications described in subsection (c)(3) of claimed infringement by such faculty member or graduate student, and such notifications of claimed infringement were not actionable under subsection (f); and

(C) the institution provides to all users of its system or network informational materials that accurately describe, and promote compliance with, the laws of the United States relating to copyright.

(2) INJUNCTIONS—For the purposes of this subsection, the limitations on injunctive relief contained in subsections (j)(2) and (j)(3), but not those in (j)(1), shall apply.

(f) MISREPRESENTATIONS—Any person who knowingly materially misrepresents under this section:

(1) that material or activity is infringing, or

(2) that material or activity was removed or disabled by mistake or misidentification, shall be liable for any damages, including costs and attorneys' fees, incurred by the alleged infringer, by any copyright owner or copyright owner's authorized licensee, or by a service provider, who is injured by such misrepresentation, as the result of the service provider relying upon such misrepresentation in removing or disabling access to the material or activity claimed to be infringing, or in replacing the removed material or ceasing to disable access to it.

(g) REPLACEMENT OF REMOVED OR DISABLED MATERIAL AND LIMITATION ON OTHER LIABILITY:

(1) NO LIABILITY FOR TAKING DOWN GENERALLY—Subject to paragraph (2), a service provider shall not be liable to any person for any claim based on the service provider's good faith disabling of access to, or removal of, material or activity claimed to be infringing or based on facts or circumstances from which infringing activity is apparent, regardless of whether the material or activity is ultimately determined to be infringing.

(2) EXCEPTION—Paragraph (1) shall not apply with respect to material residing at the direction of a subscriber of the service provider on a system or network controlled or operated by or for the service provider that is removed, or to which access is disabled by the service provider, pursuant to a notice provided under subsection (c)(1)(C), unless the service provider:

(A) takes reasonable steps promptly to notify the subscriber that it has removed or disabled access to the material;

(B) upon receipt of a counter notification described in paragraph (3), promptly provides the person who provided the notification under subsection (c)(1)(C) with a copy of the counter notification, and informs that person that it will replace the removed material or cease disabling access to it in 10 business days; and

(C) replaces the removed material and ceases disabling access to it not less than 10, nor more than 14, business days following receipt of the counter notice, unless its designated agent first receives notice from the person who submitted the notification under subsection (c)(1)(C) that such person has filed an action seeking a court order to restrain the subscriber from engaging in infringing activity relating to the material on the service provider's system or network.

(3) CONTENTS OF COUNTER NOTIFICATION- To be effective under this subsection, a counter notification must be a written communication provided to the service provider's designated agent that includes substantially the following:

(A) A physical or electronic signature of the subscriber.

(B) Identification of the material that has been removed or to which access has been disabled and the location at which the material appeared before it was removed or access to it was disabled.

(C) A statement under penalty of perjury that the subscriber has a good faith belief that the material was removed or disabled as a result of mistake or misidentification of the material to be removed or disabled.

(D) The subscriber's name, address, and telephone number, and a statement that the subscriber consents to the jurisdiction of Federal District Court for the judicial district in which the address is located, or if the subscriber's address is outside of the United States, for any judicial district in which the service provider may be found, and that the subscriber will accept service of process from the person who provided notification under subsection (c)(1)(C) or an agent of such person.

(4) LIMITATION ON OTHER LIABILITY—A service provider's compliance with paragraph (2) shall not subject the service provider to liability for copyright infringement with respect to the material identified in the notice provided under subsection (c)(1)(C).

(h) SUBPOENA TO IDENTIFY INFRINGER-

(1) REQUEST—A copyright owner or a person authorized to act on the owner's behalf may request the clerk of any United States district court to issue a subpoena to a service provider for identification of an alleged infringer in accordance with this subsection.

(2) CONTENTS OF REQUEST—The request may be made by filing with the clerk:

(A) a copy of a notification described in subsection (c)(3)(A);

(B) a proposed subpoena; and

(C) a sworn declaration to the effect that the purpose for which the subpoena is sought is to obtain the identity of an alleged infringer and that such information will only be used for the purpose of protecting rights under this title.

(3) CONTENTS OF SUBPOENA—The subpoena shall authorize and order the service provider receiving the notification and the subpoena to expeditiously disclose to the copyright owner or person authorized by the copyright owner information sufficient to identify the alleged infringer of the material described in the notification to the extent such information is available to the service provider.

(4) BASIS FOR GRANTING SUBPOENA—If the notification filed satisfies the provisions of subsection (c)(3)(A), the proposed subpoena is in proper form, and the accompanying declaration is properly executed, the clerk shall expeditiously issue and sign the proposed subpoena and return it to the requester for delivery to the service provider.

(5) ACTIONS OF SERVICE PROVIDER RECEIVING SUBPOENA—Upon receipt of the issued subpoena, either accompanying or subsequent to the receipt of a notification described in subsection (c)(3)(A), the service provider shall expeditiously disclose to the copyright owner or person authorized by the copyright owner the information required by the subpoena, notwithstanding any other provision of law and regardless of whether the service provider responds to the notification.

(6) RULES APPLICABLE TO SUBPOENA—Unless otherwise provided by this section or by applicable rules of the court, the procedure for issuance and delivery of the subpoena, and the remedies for noncompliance with the subpoena, shall be governed to the greatest extent practicable by those provisions of the Federal Rules of Civil Procedure governing the issuance, service, and enforcement of a subpoena duces tecum.

(i) CONDITIONS FOR ELIGIBILITY—

(1) ACCOMMODATION OF TECHNOLOGY—The limitations on liability established by this section shall apply to a service provider only if the service provider:

(A) has adopted and reasonably implemented, and informs subscribers and account holders of the service provider's system or network of, a policy that provides for the termination in appropriate circumstances of subscribers and account holders of the service provider's system or network who are repeat infringers; and

(B) accommodates and does not interfere with standard technical measures.

(2) DEFINITION—As used in this subsection, the term 'standard technical measures' means technical measures that are used by copyright owners to identify or protect copyrighted works and:

(A) have been developed pursuant to a broad consensus of copyright owners and service providers in an open, fair, voluntary, multi-industry standards process;

(B) are available to any person on reasonable and nondiscriminatory terms; and

(C) do not impose substantial costs on service providers or substantial burdens on their systems or networks.

(j) INJUNCTIONS—The following rules shall apply in the case of any application for an injunction under section 502 against a service provider that is not subject to monetary remedies under this section:

(1) SCOPE OF RELIEF—(A) With respect to conduct other than that which qualifies for the limitation on remedies set forth in subsection (a), the court may grant injunctive relief with respect to a service provider only in one or more of the following forms:

(i) An order restraining the service provider from providing access to infringing material or activity residing at a particular online site on the provider's system or network.

(ii) An order restraining the service provider from providing access to a subscriber or account holder of the service provider's system or network who is engaging in infringing activity and is identified in the order, by terminating the accounts of the subscriber or account holder that are specified in the order.

(iii) Such other injunctive relief as the court may consider necessary to prevent or restrain infringement of copyrighted material specified in the order of the court at a particular online location, if such relief is the least burdensome to the service provider among the forms of relief comparably effective for that purpose.

(B) If the service provider qualifies for the limitation on remedies described in subsection (a), the court may only grant injunctive relief in one or both of the following forms:

(i) An order restraining the service provider from providing access to a subscriber or account holder of the service provider's system or network who is using the provider's service to engage in infringing activity and is identified in the order, by terminating the accounts of the subscriber or account holder that are specified in the order.

(ii) An order restraining the service provider from providing access, by taking reasonable steps specified in the order to block access, to a specific, identified, online location outside the United States.

(2) CONSIDERATIONS—The court, in considering the relevant criteria for injunctive relief under applicable law, shall consider:

(A) whether such an injunction, either alone or in combination with other such injunctions issued against the same service provider under this subsection, would significantly burden either the provider or the operation of the provider's system or network;

(B) the magnitude of the harm likely to be suffered by the copyright owner in the digital network environment if steps are not taken to prevent or restrain the infringement;

'(C) whether implementation of such an injunction would be technically feasible and effective, and would not interfere with access to noninfringing material at other online locations; and

(D) whether other less burdensome and comparably effective means of preventing or restraining access to the infringing material are available.

(3) NOTICE AND EX PARTE ORDERS—Injunctive relief under this subsection shall be available only after notice to the service provider and an opportunity for the service provider to appear are provided, except for orders ensuring the preservation of evidence or other orders having no material adverse effect on the operation of the service provider's communications network.

(k) DEFINITIONS—

(1) SERVICE PROVIDER—(A) As used in subsection (a), the term 'service provider' means an entity offering the transmission, routing, or providing of connections for digital online communications, between or among points specified by a user, of material of the user's choosing, without modification to the content of the material as sent or received.

(B) As used in this section, other than subsection (a), the term 'service provider' means a provider of online services or network access, or the operator of facilities therefor, and includes an entity described in subparagraph (A).

(2) MONETARY RELIEF—As used in this section, the term 'monetary relief' means damages, costs, attorneys' fees, and any other form of monetary payment.

(l) OTHER DEFENSES NOT AFFECTED—The failure of a service provider's conduct to qualify for limitation of liability under this section shall not bear adversely upon the consideration of a defense by the service provider that the service provider's conduct is not infringing under this title or any other defense.

(m) PROTECTION OF PRIVACY- Nothing in this section shall be construed to condition the applicability of subsections (a) through (d) on:

(1) a service provider monitoring its service or affirmatively seeking facts indicating infringing activity, except to the extent consistent with a standard technical measure complying with the provisions of subsection (i); or

(2) a service provider gaining access to, removing, or disabling access to material in cases in which such conduct is prohibited by law.

(n) CONSTRUCTION—Subsections (a), (b), (c), and (d) describe separate and distinct functions for purposes of applying this section. Whether a service provider qualifies for the limitation on liability in any one of those subsections shall be based solely on the criteria in that subsection, and shall not affect a determination of whether that service provider qualifies for the limitations on liability under any other such subsection.'

(b) CONFORMING AMENDMENT—The table of sections for chapter 5 of title 17, United States Code, is amended by adding at the end the following:

512. Limitations on liability relating to material online.'.

4. SEC. 203. EFFECTIVE DATE.

This title and the amendments made by this title shall take effect on the date of the enactment of this Act.

1.   TITLE III--COMPUTER MAINTENANCE OR REPAIR COPYRIGHT EXEMPTION

5. SEC. 301. SHORT TITLE.

This title may be cited as the 'Computer Maintenance Competition Assurance Act'.

6. SEC. 302. LIMITATIONS ON EXCLUSIVE RIGHTS; COMPUTER PROGRAMS.

Section 117 of title 17, United States Code, is amended:

(1) by striking 'Notwithstanding' and inserting the following:

(a) MAKING OF ADDITIONAL COPY OR ADAPTATION BY OWNER OF COPY—Notwithstanding;

(2) by striking 'Any exact' and inserting the following:

(b) LEASE, SALE, OR OTHER TRANSFER OF ADDITIONAL COPY OR ADAPTATION—Any exact'; and

(3) by adding at the end the following:

(c) MACHINE MAINTENANCE OR REPAIR—Notwithstanding the provisions of section 106, it is not an infringement for the owner or lessee of a machine to make or authorize the making of a copy of a computer program if such copy is made solely by virtue of the activation of a machine that lawfully contains an authorized copy of the computer program, for purposes only of maintenance or repair of that machine, if:

(1) such new copy is used in no other manner and is destroyed immediately after the maintenance or repair is completed; and

(2) with respect to any computer program or part thereof that is not necessary for that machine to be activated, such program or part thereof is not accessed or used other than to make such new copy by virtue of the activation of the machine.

(d) DEFINITIONS—For purposes of this section:

(1) the 'maintenance' of a machine is the servicing of the machine in order to make it work in accordance with its original specifications and any changes to those specifications authorized for that machine; and

(2) the 'repair' of a machine is the restoring of the machine to the state of working in accordance with its original specifications and any changes to those specifications authorized for that machine.'

1. TITLE IV--MISCELLANEOUS PROVISIONS

7. SEC. 401. PROVISIONS RELATING TO THE COMMISSIONER OF PATENTS AND TRADEMARKS AND THE REGISTER OF COPYRIGHTS

(a) COMPENSATION—(1) Section 3(d) of title 35, United States Code, is amended by striking 'prescribed by law for Assistant Secretaries of Commerce' and inserting 'in effect for level III of the Executive Schedule under section 5314 of title 5, United States Code'.

(2) Section 701(e) of title 17, United States Code, is amended:

(A) by striking 'IV' and inserting 'III'; and

(B) by striking '5315' and inserting '5314'.

(3) Section 5314 of title 5, United States Code, is amended by adding at the end the following:

o 'Assistant Secretary of Commerce and Commissioner of Patents and Trademarks.'

o 'Register of Copyrights.'

(b) CLARIFICATION OF AUTHORITY OF THE COPYRIGHT OFFICE—
Section 701 of title 17, United States Code, is amended:

(1) by redesignating subsections (b) through (e) as subsections (c) through (f), respectively; and

(2) by inserting after subsection (a) the following:

(b) In addition to the functions and duties set out elsewhere in this chapter, the Register of Copyrights shall perform the following functions:

(1) Advise Congress on national and international issues relating to copyright, other matters arising under this title, and related matters.

(2) Provide information and assistance to Federal departments and agencies and the Judiciary on national and international issues relating to copyright, other matters arising under this title, and related matters.

(3) Participate in meetings of international intergovernmental organizations and meetings with foreign government officials relating to copyright, other matters arising under this title, and related matters, including as a member of United States delegations as authorized by the appropriate Executive branch authority.

(4) Conduct studies and programs regarding copyright, other matters arising under this title, and related matters, the administration of the Copyright Office, or any function vested in the Copyright Office by law, including educational programs conducted cooperatively with foreign intellectual property offices and international intergovernmental organizations.

(5) Perform such other functions as Congress may direct, or as may be appropriate in furtherance of the functions and duties specifically set forth in this title.'

8. SEC. 402. EPHEMERAL RECORDINGS.

Section 112(a) of title 17, United States Code, is amended:

(1) by redesignating paragraphs (1), (2), and (3) as subparagraphs (A), (B), and

(C), respectively;

(2) by inserting '(1)' after '(a)';

(3) by inserting after 'under a license' the following: ', including a statutory license under section 114(f),';

(4) by inserting after '114(a),' the following: 'or for a transmitting organization that is a broadcast radio or television station licensed as such by the Federal Communications Commission and that makes a broadcast transmission of a performance of a sound recording in a digital format on a nonsubscription basis,'; and

(5) by adding at the end the following:

(2) In a case in which a transmitting organization entitled to make a copy or phonorecord under paragraph (1) in connection with the transmission to the public of a performance or display of a work is prevented from making such copy or phonorecord by reason of the application by the copyright owner of technical measures that prevent the reproduction of the work, the copyright owner shall make available to the transmitting organization the necessary means for permitting the making of such copy or phonorecord as permitted under that paragraph, if it is technologically feasible and economically reasonable for the copyright owner to do so. If the copyright owner fails to do so in a timely manner in light of the transmitting organization's reasonable business requirements, the transmitting organization shall not be liable for a violation of section 1201(a)(1) of this title for engaging in such activities as are necessary to make such copies or phonorecords as permitted under paragraph (1) of this subsection.'

9. SEC. 403. LIMITATIONS ON EXCLUSIVE RIGHTS; DISTANCE EDUCATION.

(a) RECOMMENDATIONS BY REGISTER OF COPYRIGHTS—Not later than 6 months after the date of the enactment of this Act, the Register of Copyrights, after consultation with representatives of copyright owners, nonprofit educational institutions, and nonprofit libraries and archives, shall submit to the Congress recommendations on how to promote distance education through digital technologies, including interactive digital networks, while maintaining an appropriate balance between the rights of copyright owners and the needs of users of copyrighted works. Such recommendations shall include any legislation the Register of Copyrights considers appropriate to achieve the objective described in the preceding sentence.

(b) FACTORS—In formulating recommendations under subsection (a), the Register of Copyrights shall consider:

(1) the need for an exemption from exclusive rights of copyright owners for distance education through digital networks;

(2) the categories of works to be included under any distance education exemption;

(3) the extent of appropriate quantitative limitations on the portions of works that may be used under any distance education exemption;

(4) the parties who should be entitled to the benefits of any distance education exemption;

(5) the parties who should be designated as eligible recipients of distance education materials under any distance education exemption;

(6) whether and what types of technological measures can or should be employed to safeguard against unauthorized access to, and use or retention of, copyrighted materials as a condition of eligibility for any distance education exemption, including, in light of developing technological capabilities, the exemption set out in section 110(2) of title 17, United States Code;

(7) the extent to which the availability of licenses for the use of copyrighted works in distance education through interactive digital networks should be considered in assessing eligibility for any distance education exemption; and

(8) such other issues relating to distance education through interactive digital networks that the Register considers appropriate.

10. SEC. 404. EXEMPTION FOR LIBRARIES AND ARCHIVES.

Section 108 of title 17, United States Code, is amended:

(1) in subsection (a):

(A) by striking 'Notwithstanding' and inserting 'Except as otherwise provided in this title and notwithstanding';

(B) by inserting after 'no more than one copy or phonorecord of a work' the following: ', except as provided in subsections (b) and (c)'; and

(C) in paragraph (3) by inserting after 'copyright' the following: 'that appears on the copy or phonorecord that is reproduced under the provisions of this section, or includes a legend stating that the work may be protected by copyright if no such notice can be found on the copy or phonorecord that is reproduced under the provisions of this section';

(2) in subsection (b):

(A) by striking 'a copy or phonorecord' and inserting 'three copies or phonorecords';

(B) by striking 'in facsimile form'; and

(C) by striking 'if the copy or phonorecord reproduced is currently in the collections of the library or archives.' and inserting 'if:

(1) the copy or phonorecord reproduced is currently in the collections of the library or archives; and

(2) any such copy or phonorecord that is reproduced in digital format is not otherwise distributed in that format and is not made available to the public in that format outside the premises of the library or archives.'; and

(3) in subsection (c):

(A) by striking 'a copy or phonorecord' and inserting 'three copies or phonorecords';

(B) by striking 'in facsimile form';

(C) by inserting 'or if the existing format in which the work is stored has become obsolete,' after 'stolen,';

(D) by striking 'if the library or archives has, after a reasonable effort, determined that an unused replacement cannot be obtained at a fair price.' and inserting 'if:

(1) the library or archives has, after a reasonable effort, determined that an unused replacement cannot be obtained at a fair price; and

(2) any such copy or phonorecord that is reproduced in digital format is not made available to the public in that format outside the premises of the library or archives in lawful possession of such copy.'; and

(E) by adding at the end the following:

For purposes of this subsection, a format shall be considered obsolete if the machine or device necessary to render perceptible a work stored in that format is no longer manufactured or is no longer reasonably available in the commercial marketplace.'

11. SEC. 405. SCOPE OF EXCLUSIVE RIGHTS IN SOUND RECORDINGS; EPHEMERAL RECORDINGS.

(a) SCOPE OF EXCLUSIVE RIGHTS IN SOUND RECORDINGS—Section 114 of title 17, United States Code, is amended as follows:

(1) Subsection (d) is amended:

(A) in paragraph (1) by striking subparagraph (A) and inserting the following:

(A) a nonsubscription broadcast transmission;'; and

(B) by amending paragraph (2) to read as follows:

(2) STATUTORY LICENSING OF CERTAIN TRANSMISSIONS—The performance of a sound recording publicly by means of a subscription digital audio transmission not exempt under paragraph (1), an eligible nonsubscription transmission, or a transmission not exempt under paragraph (1) that is made by a preexisting satellite digital audio radio service shall be subject to statutory licensing, in accordance with subsection (f) if:

(A)(i) the transmission is not part of an interactive service;

(ii) except in the case of a transmission to a business establishment, the transmitting entity does not automatically and intentionally cause any device receiving the transmission to switch from one program channel to another; and

(iii) except as provided in section 1002(e), the transmission of the sound recording is accompanied, if technically feasible, by the information encoded in that sound recording, if any, by or under the authority of the copyright owner of that sound recording, that identifies the title of the sound recording, the featured recording artist who performs on the sound recording, and related information, including information concerning the underlying musical work and its writer;

(B) in the case of a subscription transmission not exempt under paragraph (1) that is made by a preexisting subscription service in the same transmission medium used by such service on July 31, 1998, or in the case of a transmission not exempt under paragraph (1) that is made by a preexisting satellite digital audio radio service:

(i) the transmission does not exceed the sound recording performance complement; and

(ii) the transmitting entity does not cause to be published by means of an advance program schedule or prior announcement the titles of the specific sound recordings or phonorecords embodying such sound recordings to be transmitted; and

(C) in the case of an eligible nonsubscription transmission or a subscription transmission not exempt under paragraph (1) that is made by a new subscription service or by a preexisting subscription service other than in the same transmission medium used by such service on July 31, 1998:

(i) the transmission does not exceed the sound recording performance complement, except that this requirement shall not apply in the case of a retransmission of a broadcast transmission if the retransmission is made by a transmitting entity that does not have the right or ability to control the programming of the broadcast station making the broadcast transmission, unless:

(I) the broadcast station makes broadcast transmissions:

(aa) in digital format that regularly exceed the sound recording performance complement; or

(bb) in analog format, a substantial portion of which, on a weekly basis, exceed the sound recording performance complement; and

(II) the sound recording copyright owner or its representative has notified the transmitting entity in writing that broadcast transmissions of the copyright owner's sound recordings exceed the sound recording performance complement as provided in this clause;

(ii) the transmitting entity does not cause to be published, or induce or facilitate the publication, by means of an advance program schedule or prior announcement, the titles of the specific sound recordings to be transmitted, the phonorecords embodying such sound recordings, or, other than for illustrative purposes, the names of the featured recording artists, except that this clause does not disqualify a transmitting entity that makes a prior announcement that a particular artist will be featured within an unspecified future time period, and in the case of a retransmission of a broadcast transmission by a transmitting entity that does not have the right or ability to control the programming of the broadcast transmission, the requirement of this clause shall not apply to a prior oral announcement by the broadcast station, or to an advance program schedule published, induced, or facilitated by the broadcast station, if the transmitting entity does not have actual knowledge and has not received written notice from the copyright owner or its representative that the broadcast station publishes or induces or facilitates the publication of such advance program schedule, or if such advance program schedule is a schedule of classical music programming published by the broadcast station in the same manner as published by that broadcast station on or before September 30, 1998;

(iii) the transmission:

(I) is not part of an archived program of less than 5 hours duration;

(II) is not part of an archived program of 5 hours or greater in duration that is made available for a period exceeding 2 weeks;

(III) is not part of a continuous program which is of less than 3 hours duration; or

(IV) is not part of an identifiable program in which performances of sound recordings are rendered in a predetermined order, other than an archived or continuous program, that is transmitted at:

(aa) more than 3 times in any 2-week period that have been publicly announced in advance, in the case of a program of less than 1 hour in duration, or (bb) more than 4 times in any 2-week period that have been publicly announced in advance, in the case of a program of 1 hour or more in duration, except that the requirement of this subclause shall not apply in the case of a retransmission of a broadcast transmission by a transmitting entity that does not have the right or ability to control the programming of the broadcast transmission, unless the transmitting entity is given notice in writing by the copyright owner of the sound recording that the broadcast station makes broadcast transmissions that regularly violate such requirement;

(iv) the transmitting entity does not knowingly perform the sound recording, as part of a service that offers transmissions of visual images contemporaneously with transmissions of sound recordings, in a manner that is likely to cause confusion, to cause mistake, or to deceive, as to the affiliation, connection, or association of the copyright owner or featured recording artist with the transmitting entity or a particular product or service advertised by the transmitting entity, or as to the origin, sponsorship, or approval by the copyright owner or featured recording artist of the activities of the transmitting entity other than the performance of the sound recording itself;

(v) the transmitting entity cooperates to prevent, to the extent feasible without imposing substantial costs or burdens, a transmission recipient or any other person or entity from automatically scanning the transmitting entity's transmissions alone or together with transmissions by other transmitting entities in order to select a particular sound recording to be transmitted to the transmission recipient, except that the requirement of this clause shall not apply to a satellite digital audio service that is in operation, or that is licensed by the Federal Communications Commission, on or before July 31, 1998;

(vi) the transmitting entity takes no affirmative steps to cause or induce the making of a phonorecord by the transmission recipient, and if the technology used by the transmitting entity enables the transmitting entity to limit the making by the transmission recipient of phonorecords of the transmission directly in a digital format, the transmitting entity sets such technology to limit such making of phonorecords to the extent permitted by such technology;

(vii) phonorecords of the sound recording have been distributed to the public under the authority of the copyright owner or the copyright owner authorizes the transmitting entity to transmit the sound recording, and the transmitting entity makes the transmission from a phonorecord lawfully made under the authority of the copyright owner, except that the requirement of this clause shall not apply to a retransmission of a broadcast transmission by a transmitting entity that does not have the right or ability to control the programming of the broadcast transmission, unless the transmitting entity is given notice in writing by the copyright owner of the sound recording that the broadcast station makes broadcast transmissions that regularly violate such requirement;

(viii) the transmitting entity accommodates and does not interfere with the transmission of technical measures that are widely used by sound recording copyright owners to identify or protect copyrighted works, and that are technically feasible of being transmitted by the transmitting entity without imposing substantial costs on the transmitting entity or resulting in perceptible aural or visual degradation of the digital signal, except that the requirement of this clause shall not apply to a satellite digital audio service that is in operation, or that is licensed under the authority of the Federal Communications Commission, on or before July 31, 1998, to the extent that such service has designed, developed, or made commitments to procure equipment or technology that is not compatible with such technical measures before such technical measures are widely adopted by sound recording copyright owners; and

(ix) the transmitting entity identifies in textual data the sound recording during, but not before, the time it is performed, including the title of the sound recording, the title of the phonorecord embodying such sound recording, if any, and the featured recording artist, in a manner to permit it to be displayed to the transmission recipient by the device or technology intended for receiving the service provided by the transmitting entity, except that the obligation in this clause shall not take effect until 1 year after the date of the enactment of the Digital Millennium Copyright Act and shall not apply in the case of a retransmission of a broadcast transmission by a transmitting entity that does not have the right or ability to control the programming of the broadcast transmission, or in the case in which devices or technology intended for receiving the service provided by the transmitting entity that have the capability to display such textual data are not common in the marketplace.'

(2) Subsection (f) is amended:

(A) in the subsection heading by striking 'NONEXEMPT SUBSCRIPTION' and inserting 'CERTAIN NONEXEMPT';

(B) in paragraph (1):

(i) in the first sentence:

(I) by striking '(1) No' and inserting '(1)(A) No';

(II) by striking 'the activities' and inserting 'subscription transmissions by preexisting subscription services and transmissions by preexisting satellite digital audio radio services'; and

(III) by striking '2000' and inserting '2001'; and

(ii) by amending the third sentence to read as follows: 'Any copyright owners of sound recordings, preexisting subscription services, or preexisting satellite digital audio radio services may submit to the Librarian of Congress licenses covering such subscription transmissions with respect to such sound recordings.'; and

(C) by striking paragraphs (2), (3), (4), and (5) and inserting the following:

(B) In the absence of license agreements negotiated under subparagraph (A), during the 60-day period commencing 6 months after publication of the notice specified in subparagraph (A), and upon the filing of a petition in accordance with section 803(a)(1), the Librarian of Congress shall, pursuant to chapter 8, convene a copyright arbitration royalty panel to determine and publish in the Federal Register a schedule of rates and terms which, subject to paragraph (3), shall be binding on all copyright owners of sound recordings and entities performing sound recordings affected by this paragraph. In establishing rates and terms for preexisting subscription services and preexisting satellite digital audio radio services, in addition to the objectives set forth in section 801(b)(1), the copyright arbitration royalty panel may consider the rates and terms for comparable types of subscription digital audio transmission services and comparable circumstances under voluntary license agreements negotiated as provided in subparagraph (A).

(C) (i) Publication of a notice of the initiation of voluntary negotiation proceedings as specified in subparagraph (A) shall be repeated, in accordance with regulations that the Librarian of Congress shall prescribe--

(I) no later than 30 days after a petition is filed by any copyright owners of sound recordings, any preexisting subscription services, or any preexisting satellite digital audio radio services indicating that a new type of subscription digital audio transmission service on which sound recordings are performed is or is about to become operational; and

(II) in the first week of January 2001, and at 5-year intervals thereafter.

(ii) The procedures specified in subparagraph (B) shall be repeated, in accordance with regulations that the Librarian of Congress shall prescribe, upon filing of a petition in accordance with section 803(a)(1) during a 60-day period commencing:

(I) 6 months after publication of a notice of the initiation of voluntary negotiation proceedings under subparagraph (A) pursuant to a petition under clause (i)(I) of this subparagraph; or

(II) on July 1, 2001, and at 5-year intervals thereafter.

(iii) The procedures specified in subparagraph (B) shall be concluded in accordance with section 802.

(2) (A) No later than 30 days after the date of the enactment of the Digital Millennium Copyright Act, the Librarian of Congress shall cause notice to be published in the Federal Register of the initiation of voluntary negotiation proceedings for the purpose of determining reasonable terms and rates of royalty payments for public performances of sound recordings by means of eligible nonsubscription transmissions and transmissions by new subscription services specified by subsection (d)(2) during the period beginning on the date of the enactment of such Act and ending on December 31, 2000, or such other date as the parties may agree. Such rates and terms shall distinguish among the different types of eligible nonsubscription transmission services and new subscription services then in operation and shall include a minimum fee for each such type of service. Any copyright owners of sound recordings or any entities performing sound recordings affected by this paragraph may submit to the Librarian of Congress licenses covering such eligible nonsubscription transmissions and new subscription services with respect to such sound recordings. The parties to each negotiation proceeding shall bear their own costs.

(B) In the absence of license agreements negotiated under subparagraph (A), during the 60-day period commencing 6 months after publication of the notice specified in subparagraph (A), and upon the filing of a petition in accordance with section 803(a)(1), the Librarian of Congress shall, pursuant to chapter 8, convene a copyright arbitration royalty panel to determine and publish in the Federal Register a schedule of rates and terms which, subject to paragraph (3), shall be binding on all copyright owners of sound recordings and entities performing sound recordings affected by this paragraph during the period beginning on the date of the enactment of the Digital Millennium Copyright Act and ending on December 31, 2000, or such other date as the parties may agree. Such rates and terms shall distinguish among the different types of eligible nonsubscription transmission services then in operation and shall include a minimum fee for each such type of service, such differences to be based on criteria including, but not limited to, the quantity and nature of the use of sound recordings and the degree to which use of the service may substitute for or may promote the purchase of phonorecords by consumers. In establishing rates and terms for transmissions by eligible nonsubscription services and new subscription services, the copyright arbitration royalty panel shall establish rates and terms that most clearly represent the rates and terms that would have been negotiated in the marketplace between a willing buyer and a willing seller. In determining such rates and terms, the copyright arbitration royalty panel shall base its decision on economic, competitive and programming information presented by the parties, including:

(i) whether use of the service may substitute for or may promote the sales of phonorecords or otherwise may interfere with or may enhance the sound recording copyright owner's other streams of revenue from its sound recordings; and

(ii) the relative roles of the copyright owner and the transmitting entity in the copyrighted work and the service made available to the public with respect to relative creative contribution, technological contribution, capital investment, cost, and risk.

In establishing such rates and terms, the copyright arbitration royalty panel may consider the rates and terms for comparable types of digital audio transmission services and comparable circumstances under voluntary license agreements negotiated under subparagraph (A).

(C) (i) Publication of a notice of the initiation of voluntary negotiation proceedings as specified in subparagraph (A) shall be repeated in accordance with regulations that the Librarian of Congress shall prescribe:

(I) no later than 30 days after a petition is filed by any copyright owners of sound recordings or any eligible nonsubscription service or new subscription service indicating that a new type of eligible nonsubscription service or new subscription service on which sound recordings are performed is or is about to become operational; and

(II) in the first week of January 2000, and at 2-year intervals thereafter, except to the extent that different years for the repeating of such proceedings may be determined in accordance with subparagraph (A).

(ii) The procedures specified in subparagraph (B) shall be repeated, in accordance with regulations that the Librarian of Congress shall prescribe, upon filing of a petition in accordance with section 803(a)(1) during a 60-day period commencing:

(I) 6 months after publication of a notice of the initiation of voluntary negotiation proceedings under subparagraph (A) pursuant to a petition under clause (i)(I); or

(II) on July 1, 2000, and at 2-year intervals thereafter, except to the extent that different years for the repeating of such proceedings may be determined in accordance with subparagraph (A).

(iii) The procedures specified in subparagraph (B) shall be concluded in accordance with section 802.

(3) License agreements voluntarily negotiated at any time between 1 or

more copyright owners of sound recordings and 1 or more entities performing sound recordings shall be given effect in lieu of any determination by a copyright arbitration royalty panel or decision by the Librarian of Congress.

(4) (A) The Librarian of Congress shall also establish requirements by which copyright owners may receive reasonable notice of the use of their sound recordings under this section, and under which records of such use shall be kept and made available by entities performing sound recordings.

(B) Any person who wishes to perform a sound recording publicly by means of a transmission eligible for statutory licensing under this subsection may do so without infringing the exclusive right of the copyright owner of the sound recording:

(i) by complying with such notice requirements as the Librarian of Congress shall prescribe by regulation and by paying royalty fees in accordance with this subsection; or

(ii) if such royalty fees have not been set, by agreeing to pay such royalty fees as shall be determined in accordance with this subsection.

(C) Any royalty payments in arrears shall be made on or before the twentieth day of the month next succeeding the month in which the royalty fees are set.'

(3) Subsection (g) is amended:

(A) in the subsection heading by striking 'SUB-SCRIPTION;'

(B) in paragraph (1) in the matter preceding subparagraph (A), by striking 'subscription transmission licensed' and inserting 'transmission licensed under a statutory license;'

(C) in subparagraphs (A) and (B) by striking 'subscription'; and

(D) in paragraph (2) by striking 'subscription.'

(4) Subsection (j) is amended:

(A) by striking paragraphs (4) and (9) and redesignating paragraphs (2), (3), (5), (6), (7), and (8) as paragraphs (3), (5), (9), (12), (13), and (14), respectively;

(B) by inserting after paragraph (1) the following:

(2) An 'archived program' is a predetermined program that is available repeatedly on the demand of the transmission recipient and that is performed in the same order from the beginning, except that an archived program shall not include a recorded event or broadcast transmission that makes no more than an incidental use of sound recordings, as long as such recorded event or broadcast transmission does not contain an entire sound recording or feature a particular sound recording.'

(C) by inserting after paragraph (3), as so redesignated, the following:

(4) A 'continuous program' is a predetermined program that is continuously

performed in the same order and that is accessed at a point in the program that is beyond the control of the transmission recipient.'

(D) by inserting after paragraph (5), as so redesignated, the following:

(6) An 'eligible nonsubscription transmission' is a noninteractive nonsubscription digital audio transmission not exempt under subsection (d)(1) that is made as part of a service that provides audio programming consisting, in whole or in part, of performances of sound recordings, including retransmissions of broadcast transmissions, if the primary purpose of the service is to provide to the public such audio or other entertainment programming, and the primary purpose of the service is not to sell, advertise, or promote particular products or services other than sound recordings, live concerts, or other music-related events.

(7) An 'interactive service' is one that enables a member of the public to receive a transmission of a program specially created for the recipient, or on request, a transmission of a particular sound recording, whether or not as part of a program, which is selected by or on behalf of the recipient. The ability of individuals to request that particular sound recordings be performed for reception by the public at large, or in the case of a subscription service, by all subscribers of the service, does not make a service interactive, if the programming on each channel of the service does not substantially consist of sound recordings that are performed within 1 hour of the request or at a time designated by either the transmitting entity or the individual making such request. If an entity offers both interactive and noninteractive services (either concurrently or at different times), the noninteractive component shall not be treated as part of an interactive service.

(8) A 'new subscription service' is a service that performs sound recordings by means of noninteractive subscription digital audio transmissions and that is not a preexisting subscription service or a preexisting satellite digital audio radio service.'

(E) by inserting after paragraph (9), as so redesignated, the following:

(10) A 'preexisting satellite digital audio radio service' is a subscription satellite digital audio radio service provided pursuant to a satellite digital audio radio service license issued by the Federal Communications Commission on or before July 31, 1998, and any renewal of such license to the extent of the scope of the original license, and may include a limited number of sample channels representative of the subscription service that are made available on a nonsubscription basis in order to promote the subscription service.

(11) A 'preexisting subscription service' is a service that performs sound recordings by means of noninteractive audio-only subscription digital audio

transmissions, which was in existence and was making such transmissions to the public for a fee on or before July 31, 1998, and may include a limited number of sample channels representative of the subscription service that are made available on a nonsubscription basis in order to promote the subscription service.'; and

(F) by adding at the end the following:

(15) A 'transmission' is either an initial transmission or a retransmission.'

(5) The amendment made by paragraph (2)(B)(i)(III) of this subsection shall be deemed to have been enacted as part of the Digital Performance Right in Sound Recordings Act of 1995, and the publication of notice of proceedings under section 114(f)(1) of title 17, United States Code, as in effect upon the effective date of that Act, for the determination of royalty payments shall be deemed to have been made for the period beginning on the effective date of that Act and ending on December 1, 2001.

(6) The amendments made by this subsection do not annul, limit, or otherwise impair the rights that are preserved by section 114 of title 17, United States Code, including the rights preserved by subsections (c), (d)(4), and (i) of such section.

(b) EPHEMERAL RECORDINGS- Section 112 of title 17, United States Code, is amended:

(1) by redesignating subsection (e) as subsection (f); and

(2) by inserting after subsection (d) the following:

(e) STATUTORY LICENSE: (1) A transmitting organization entitled to transmit to the public a performance of a sound recording under the limitation on exclusive rights specified by section 114(d)(1)(C)(iv) or under a statutory license in accordance with section 114(f) is entitled to a statutory license, under the conditions specified by this subsection, to make no more than 1 phonorecord of the sound recording (unless the terms and conditions of the statutory license allow for more), if the following conditions are satisfied:

(A) The phonorecord is retained and used solely by the transmitting organization that made it, and no further phonorecords are reproduced from it.

(B) The phonorecord is used solely for the transmitting organization's own transmissions originating in the United States under a statutory license in accordance with section 114(f) or the limitation on exclusive rights specified by section 114(d)(1)(C)(iv).

(C) Unless preserved exclusively for purposes of archival preservation, the phonorecord is destroyed within 6 months from the date the sound recording was first transmitted to the public using the phonorecord.

(D) Phonorecords of the sound recording have been distributed to the public under the authority of the copyright owner or the copyright owner authorizes the transmitting entity to transmit the sound recording, and the transmitting entity makes the phonorecord under this subsection from a phonorecord lawfully made and acquired under the authority of the copyright owner.

(3) Notwithstanding any provision of the antitrust laws, any copyright owners of sound recordings and any transmitting organizations entitled to a statutory license under this subsection may negotiate and agree upon royalty rates and license terms and conditions for making phonorecords of such sound recordings under this section and the proportionate division of fees paid among copyright owners, and may designate common agents to negotiate, agree to, pay, or receive such royalty payments.

(4) No later than 30 days after the date of the enactment of the Digital Millennium Copyright Act, the Librarian of Congress shall cause notice to be published in the Federal Register of the initiation of voluntary negotiation proceedings for the purpose of determining reasonable terms and rates of royalty payments for the activities specified by paragraph (2) of this subsection during the period beginning on the date of the enactment of such Act and ending on December 31, 2000, or such other date as the parties may agree. Such rates shall include a minimum fee for each type of service offered by transmitting organizations. Any copyright owners of sound recordings or any transmitting organizations entitled to a statutory license under this subsection may submit to the Librarian of Congress licenses covering such activities with respect to such sound recordings. The parties to each negotiation proceeding shall bear their own costs.

(5) In the absence of license agreements negotiated under paragraph (3), during the 60-day period commencing 6 months after publication of the notice specified in paragraph (4), and upon the filing of a petition in accordance with section 803(a) (1), the Librarian of Congress shall, pursuant to chapter 8, convene a copyright arbitration royalty panel to determine and publish in the Federal Register a schedule of reasonable rates and terms which, subject to paragraph (6), shall be binding on all copyright owners of sound recordings and transmitting organizations entitled to a statutory license under this subsection during the period beginning on the date of the enactment of the Digital Millennium Copyright Act and ending on December 31, 2000, or such other date as the parties may agree. Such rates shall include a minimum fee for each type of service offered by transmitting organizations. The copyright arbitration royalty panel shall establish rates that most clearly represent the fees that would have been negotiated in the marketplace between a willing buyer and a willing seller. In determining such rates and terms, the copyright arbitration royalty panel

shall base its decision on economic, competitive, and programming information presented by the parties, including:

(A) whether use of the service may substitute for or may promote the sales of phonorecords or otherwise interferes with or enhances the copyright owner's traditional streams of revenue; and

(B) the relative roles of the copyright owner and the transmitting organization in the copyrighted work and the service made available to the public with respect to relative creative contribution, technological contribution, capital investment, cost, and risk.

In establishing such rates and terms, the copyright arbitration royalty panel may consider the rates and terms under voluntary license agreements negotiated as provided in paragraphs (3) and (4). The Librarian of Congress shall also establish requirements by which copyright owners may receive reasonable notice of the use of their sound recordings under this section, and under which records of such use shall be kept and made available by transmitting organizations entitled to obtain a statutory license under this subsection.

(6) License agreements voluntarily negotiated at any time between 1 or more copyright owners of sound recordings and 1 or more transmitting organizations entitled to obtain a statutory license under this subsection shall be given effect in lieu of any determination by a copyright arbitration royalty panel or decision by the Librarian of Congress.

(7) Publication of a notice of the initiation of voluntary negotiation proceedings as specified in paragraph (4) shall be repeated, in accordance with regulations that the Librarian of Congress shall prescribe, in the first week of January 2000, and at 2-year intervals thereafter, except to the extent that different years for the repeating of such proceedings may be determined in accordance with paragraph (4). The procedures specified in paragraph (5) shall be repeated, in accordance with regulations that the Librarian of Congress shall prescribe, upon filing of a petition in accordance with section 803(a)(1), during a 60-day period commencing on July 1, 2000, and at 2-year intervals thereafter, except to the extent that different years for the repeating of such proceedings may be determined in accordance with paragraph (4). The procedures specified in paragraph (5) shall be concluded in accordance with section 802.

(8)(A) Any person who wishes to make a phonorecord of a sound recording under a statutory license in accordance with this subsection may do so without infringing the exclusive right of the copyright owner of the sound recording under section 106(1):

(i) by complying with such notice requirements as the Librarian of Congress shall prescribe by regulation and by paying royalty fees in accordance with this subsection; or

(ii) if such royalty fees have not been set, by agreeing to pay such royalty fees as shall be determined in accordance with this subsection.

(B) Any royalty payments in arrears shall be made on or before the 20th day of the month next succeeding the month in which the royalty fees are set.

(9) If a transmitting organization entitled to make a phonorecord under this subsection is prevented from making such phonorecord by reason of the application by the copyright owner of technical measures that prevent the reproduction of the sound recording, the copyright owner shall make available to the transmitting organization the necessary means for permitting the making of such phonorecord as permitted under this subsection, if it is technologically feasible and economically reasonable for the copyright owner to do so. If the copyright owner fails to do so in a timely manner in light of the transmitting organization's reasonable business requirements, the transmitting organization shall not be liable for a violation of section 1201(a)(1) of this title for engaging in such activities as are necessary to make such phonorecords as permitted under this subsection.

(10) Nothing in this subsection annuls, limits, impairs, or otherwise affects in any way the existence or value of any of the exclusive rights of the copyright owners in a sound recording, except as otherwise provided in this subsection, or in a musical work, including the exclusive rights to reproduce and distribute a sound recording or musical work, including by means of a digital phonorecord delivery, under sections 106(1), 106(3), and 115, and the right to perform publicly a sound recording or musical work, including by means of a digital audio transmission, under sections 106(4) and 106(6).'

(c) SCOPE OF SECTION 112(a) OF TITLE 17 NOT AFFECTED- Nothing in this section or the amendments made by this section shall affect the scope of section 112(a) of title 17, United States Code, or the entitlement of any person to an exemption thereunder.

(d) PROCEDURAL AMENDMENTS TO CHAPTER 8- Section 802 of title 17, United States Code, is amended:

(1) in subsection (f):

(A) in the first sentence by striking '60' and inserting '90'; and

(B) in the third sentence by striking 'that 60-day period' and inserting 'an additional 30-day period'; and

(2) in subsection (g) by inserting after the second sentence the following: 'When this title provides that the royalty rates or terms that were previously in effect are to expire on a specified date, any adjustment by the Librarian of those rates or terms shall be effective as of the day following the date of expiration of the rates or terms that were previously in effect, even if the Librarian's decision is rendered on a later date.'

(e) CONFORMING AMENDMENTS—(1) Section 801(b)(1) of title 17, United States Code, is amended in the second sentence by striking 'sections 114, 115, and 116' and inserting 'sections 114(f)(1)(B), 115, and 116.'

(2) Section 802(c) of title 17, United States Code, is amended by striking 'section 111, 114, 116, or 119, any person entitled to a compulsory license' and inserting 'section 111, 112, 114, 116, or 119, any transmitting organization entitled to a statutory license under section 112(f), any person entitled to a statutory license.'

(3) Section 802(g) of title 17, United States Code, is amended by striking 'sections 111, 114' and inserting 'sections 111, 112, 114.'

(4) Section 802(h)(2) of title 17, United States Code, is amended by striking 'section 111, 114' and inserting 'section 111, 112, 114.'

(5) Section 803(a)(1) of title 17, United States Code, is amended by striking 'sections 114, 115' and inserting 'sections 112, 114, 115.'

(6) Section 803(a)(5) of title 17, United States Code, is amended:

(A) by striking 'section 114' and inserting 'section 112 or 114;' and

(B) by striking 'that section' and inserting 'those sections.'

12. SEC. 406. ASSUMPTION OF CONTRACTUAL OBLIGATIONS RELATED TO TRANSFERS OF RIGHTS IN MOTION PICTURES.

(a) IN GENERAL- Part VI of title 28, United States Code, is amended by adding at the end the following new chapter:

2. CHAPTER 180—ASSUMPTION OF CERTAIN CONTRACTUAL OBLIGATIONS.

Sec. 4001. Assumption of contractual obligations related to transfers of rights in motion pictures.

1. Sec. 4001. Assumption of contractual obligations related to transfers of rights in motion pictures.

(a) ASSUMPTION OF OBLIGATIONS— (1) In the case of a transfer of copyright ownership under United States law in a motion picture (as the terms 'transfer of copyright ownership' and 'motion picture' are defined in section 101 of title 17) that is produced subject to 1 or more collective bargaining agreements negotiated under the laws of the United States, if the transfer is executed on or after the effective date of this chapter and is not limited to public performance rights, the transfer instrument shall be deemed to incorporate the assumption agreements applicable to the copyright ownership being transferred that are required by the applicable collective bargaining agreement, and the transferee shall be subject to the obligations under each such assumption agreement to make residual payments and provide related notices, accruing after the effective date of the transfer and applicable to the exploitation of the rights transferred, and any remedies under each such assumption agreement for breach of those obligations, as those obligations and remedies are set forth in the applicable collective bargaining agreement, if:

(A) the transferee knows or has reason to know at the time of the transfer that such collective bargaining agreement was or will be applicable to the motion picture; or

(B) in the event of a court order confirming an arbitration award against the transferor under the collective bargaining agreement, the transferor does not have the financial ability to satisfy the award within 90 days after the order is issued.

(2) For purposes of paragraph (1)(A), 'knows or has reason to know' means any of the following:

(A) Actual knowledge that the collective bargaining agreement was or will be applicable to the motion picture.

(B)(i) Constructive knowledge that the collective bargaining agreement was or will be applicable to the motion picture, arising from recordation of a document pertaining to copyright in the motion picture under section 205 of title 17 or from publication, at a site available to the public on-line that is operated by the relevant union, of information that identifies the motion picture as subject to a collective bargaining agreement with that union, if the site permits commercially reasonable verification of the date on which the information was available for access.

(ii) Clause (i) applies only if the transfer referred to in subsection (a)(1) occurs:

(I) after the motion picture is completed, or

(II) before the motion picture is completed and:

(aa) within 18 months before the filing of an application for copyright registration for the motion picture under section 408 of title 17, or

(bb) if no such application is filed, within 18 months before the first publication of the motion picture in the United States.

(C) Awareness of other facts and circumstances pertaining to a particular transfer from which it is apparent that the collective bargaining agreement was or will be applicable to the motion picture.

(b) SCOPE OF EXCLUSION OF TRANSFERS OF PUBLIC PERFORMANCE RIGHTS—For purposes of this section, the exclusion under subsection (a) of transfers of copyright ownership in a motion picture that are limited to public performance rights includes transfers to a terrestrial broadcast station, cable system, or programmer to the extent that the station, system, or programmer is functioning as an exhibitor of the motion picture, either by exhibiting the motion picture on its own network, system, service, or station, or by initiating the transmission of an exhibition that is carried on another network, system, service, or station. When a terrestrial broadcast station, cable system, or programmer, or other transferee, is also functioning otherwise as a distributor or as a producer of the motion picture, the public performance exclusion does not affect any obligations imposed on the transferee to the extent that it is engaging in such functions.

(c) EXCLUSION FOR GRANTS OF SECURITY INTERESTS—Subsection (a) shall not apply to:

(1) a transfer of copyright ownership consisting solely of a mortgage, hypothecation, or other security interest; or

(2) a subsequent transfer of the copyright ownership secured by the security interest described in paragraph (1) by or under the authority of the secured party, including a transfer through the exercise of the secured party's rights or remedies as a secured party, or by a subsequent transferee.

The exclusion under this subsection shall not affect any rights or remedies under law or contract.

(d) DEFERRAL PENDING RESOLUTION OF BONA FIDE DISPUTE—A transferee on which obligations are imposed under subsection (a) by virtue of paragraph (1) of that subsection may elect to defer performance of such obligations that are subject to a bona fide dispute between a union and a prior transferor until that dispute is resolved, except that such deferral shall not stay accrual of any union claims due under an applicable collective bargaining agreement.

(e) SCOPE OF OBLIGATIONS DETERMINED BY PRIVATE AGREEMENT—Nothing in this section shall expand or diminish the rights, obligations, or remedies of any person under the collective bargaining agreements or assumption agreements referred to in this section.

(f) FAILURE TO NOTIFY—If the transferor under subsection (a) fails to notify the transferee under subsection (a) of applicable collective bargaining obligations before the execution of the transfer instrument, and subsection (a) is made applicable to the transferee solely by virtue of subsection (a)(1)(B), the transferor shall be liable to the transferee for any damages suffered by the transferee as a result of the failure to notify.

(g) DETERMINATION OF DISPUTES AND CLAIMS—Any dispute concerning the application of subsections (a) through (f) shall be determined by an action in United States district court, and the court in its discretion may allow the recovery of full costs by or against any party and may also award a reasonable attorney's fee to the prevailing party as part of the costs.

(h) STUDY—The Comptroller General, in consultation with the Register of Copyrights, shall conduct a study of the conditions in the motion picture industry that gave rise to this section, and the impact of this section on the motion picture industry. The Comptroller General shall report the findings of the study to the Congress within 2 years after the effective date of this chapter.'

(b) CONFORMING AMENDMENT—The table of chapters for part VI of title 28, United States Code, is amended by adding at the end the following:

4001'. SEC. 407. EFFECTIVE DATE.

Except as otherwise provided in this title, this title and the amendments made by this title shall take effect on the date of the enactment of this Act.

2. TITLE V—PROTECTION OF CERTAIN ORIGINAL DESIGNS

1. SEC. 501. SHORT TITLE.
This Act may be referred to as the 'Vessel Hull Design Protection Act'.

2. SEC. 502. PROTECTION OF CERTAIN ORIGINAL DESIGNS.
Title 17, United States Code, is amended by adding at the end the following new chapter:

3. CHAPTER 13--PROTECTION OF ORIGINAL DESIGNS
Sec.
1301. Designs protected.
1302. Designs not subject to protection

1. Sec. 1301. Designs protected:

(a) DESIGNS PROTECTED—

(1) IN GENERAL—The designer or other owner of an original design of a useful article which makes the article attractive or distinctive in appearance to the purchasing or using public may secure the protection provided by this chapter upon

complying with and subject to this chapter.

(2) VESSEL HULLS—The design of a vessel hull, including a plug or mold, is subject to protection under this chapter, notwithstanding section 1302(4).

(b) DEFINITIONS—For the purpose of this chapter, the following terms have the following meanings:

(1) A design is 'original' if it is the result of the designer's creative endeavor that provides a distinguishable variation over prior work pertaining to similar articles which is more than merely trivial and has not been copied from another source.

(2) A 'useful article' is a vessel hull, including a plug or mold, which in normal use has an intrinsic utilitarian function that is not merely to portray the appearance of the article or to convey information. An article which normally is part of a useful article shall be deemed to be a useful article.

(3) A 'vessel' is a craft, especially one larger than a rowboat, designed to navigate on water, but does not include any such craft that exceeds 200 feet in length.

(4) A 'hull' is the frame or body of a vessel, including the deck of a vessel, exclusive of masts, sails, yards, and rigging.

(5) A 'plug' means a device or model used to make a mold for the purpose of exact duplication, regardless of whether the device or model has an intrinsic utilitarian function that is not only to portray the appearance of the product or to convey information.

(6) A 'mold' means a matrix or form in which a substance for material is used, regardless of whether the matrix or form has an intrinsic utilitarian function that is not only to portray the appearance of the product or to convey information.

2. Sec. 1302. Designs not subject to protection:

Protection under this chapter shall not be available for a design that is:

(1) not original;

(2) staple or commonplace, such as a standard geometric figure, a familiar symbol, an emblem, or a motif, or another shape, pattern, or configuration which has become standard, common, prevalent, or ordinary;

(3) different from a design excluded by paragraph (2) only in insignificant details or in elements which are variants commonly used in the relevant trades;

(4) dictated solely by a utilitarian function of the article that embodies it; or

(5) embodied in a useful article that was made public by the designer or owner in the United States or a foreign country more than 1 year before the date of the application for registration under this chapter.

3.   Sec. 1303. Revisions, adaptations, and rearrangements:

Protection for a design under this chapter shall be available notwithstanding the employment in the design of subject matter excluded from protection under section 1302 if the design is a substantial revision, adaptation, or rearrangement of such subject matter. Such protection shall be independent of any subsisting protection in subject matter employed in the design, and shall not be construed as securing any right to subject matter excluded from protection under this chapter or as extending any subsisting protection under this chapter.

4.   Sec. 1304. Commencement of protection:

The protection provided for a design under this chapter shall commence upon the earlier of the date of publication of the registration under section 1313(a) or the date the design is first made public as defined by section 1310(b).

5.   Sec. 1305. Term of protection:

(a) IN GENERAL—Subject to subsection (b), the protection provided under this chapter for a design shall continue for a term of 10 years beginning on the date of the commencement of protection under section 1304.

(b) EXPIRATION—All terms of protection provided in this section shall run to the end of the calendar year in which they would otherwise expire.

(c) TERMINATION OF RIGHTS—Upon expiration or termination of protection in a particular design under this chapter, all rights under this chapter in the design shall terminate, regardless of the number of different articles in which the design may have been used during the term of its protection.

6.   Sec. 1306. Design notice:

(a) CONTENTS OF DESIGN NOTICE— (1) Whenever any design for which protection is sought under this chapter is made public under section 1310(b), the owner of the design shall, subject to the provisions of section 1307, mark it or have it marked legibly with a design notice consisting of:

(A) the words 'Protected Design', the abbreviation 'Prot'd Des.,' or the letter 'D' with a circle, or the symbol '*D*;'

(B) the year of the date on which protection for the design commenced; and

(C) the name of the owner, an abbreviation by which the name can be recognized, or a generally accepted alternative designation of the owner.

Any distinctive identification of the owner may be used for purposes of subparagraph (C) if it has been recorded by the Administrator before the design marked with such identification is registered.

(2) After registration, the registration number may be used instead of the elements specified in subparagraphs (B) and (C) of paragraph (1).

(b) LOCATION OF NOTICE—The design notice shall be so located and applied as to give reasonable notice of design protection while the useful article embodying the design is passing through its normal channels of commerce.

(c) SUBSEQUENT REMOVAL OF NOTICE- When the owner of a design has complied with the provisions of this section, protection under this chapter shall not be affected by the removal, destruction, or obliteration by others of the design notice on an article.

7. Sec. 1307. Effect of omission of notice:

(a) ACTIONS WITH NOTICE—Except as provided in subsection (b), the omission of the notice prescribed in section 1306 shall not cause loss of the protection under this chapter or prevent recovery for infringement under this chapter against any person who, after receiving written notice of the design protection, begins an undertaking leading to infringement under this chapter.

(b) ACTIONS WITHOUT NOTICE—The omission of the notice prescribed in section 1306 shall prevent any recovery under section 1323 against a person who began an undertaking leading to infringement under this chapter before receiving written notice of the design protection. No injunction shall be issued under this chapter with respect to such undertaking unless the owner of the design reimburses that person for any reasonable expenditure or contractual obligation in connection with such undertaking that was incurred before receiving written notice of the design protection, as the court in its discretion directs. The burden of providing written notice of design protection shall be on the owner of the design.

8. Sec. 1308. Exclusive rights:

The owner of a design protected under this chapter has the exclusive right to:

(1) make, have made, or import, for sale or for use in trade, any useful article embodying that design; and

(2) sell or distribute for sale or for use in trade any useful article embodying that design.

9.   **Sec. 1309. Infringement:**

(a) ACTS OF INFRINGEMENT—Except as provided in subsection (b), it shall be infringement of the exclusive rights in a design protected under this chapter for any person, without the consent of the owner of the design, within the United States and during the term of such protection, to:

(1) make, have made, or import, for sale or for use in trade, any infringing article as defined in subsection (e); or

(2) sell or distribute for sale or for use in trade any such infringing article.

(b) ACTS OF SELLERS AND DISTRIBUTORS—A seller or distributor of an infringing article who did not make or import the article shall be deemed to have infringed on a design protected under this chapter only if that person:

(1) induced or acted in collusion with a manufacturer to make, or an importer to import such article, except that merely purchasing or giving an order to purchase such article in the ordinary course of business shall not of itself constitute such inducement or collusion; or

(2) refused or failed, upon the request of the owner of the design, to make a prompt and full disclosure of that person's source of such article, and that person orders or reorders such article after receiving notice by registered or certified mail of the protection subsisting in the design.

(c) ACTS WITHOUT KNOWLEDGE—It shall not be infringement under this section to make, have made, import, sell, or distribute, any article embodying a design which was created without knowledge that a design was protected under this chapter and was copied from such protected design.

(d) ACTS IN ORDINARY COURSE OF BUSINESS—A person who incorporates into that person's product of manufacture an infringing article acquired from others in the ordinary course of business, or who, without knowledge of the protected design embodied in an infringing article, makes or processes the infringing article for the account of another person in the ordinary course of business, shall not be deemed to have infringed the rights in that design under this chapter except under a condition contained in paragraph (1) or (2) of subsection (b). Accepting an order or reorder from the source of the infringing article shall be deemed ordering or reordering within the meaning of subsection (b)(2).

(e) INFRINGING ARTICLE DEFINED—As used in this section, an 'infringing article' is any article the design of which has been copied from a design protected under this chapter, without the consent of the owner of the protected design. An infringing article is not an illustration or picture of a protected design in an advertisement, book, periodical, newspaper, photograph, broadcast, motion picture, or similar medium. A design shall not be deemed to have been copied from a protected design if it is original and not substantially similar in appearance to a protected design.

(f) ESTABLISHING ORIGINALITY—The party to any action or proceeding under this chapter who alleges rights under this chapter in a design shall have the burden of establishing the design's originality whenever the opposing party introduces an earlier work which is identical to such design, or so similar as to make prima facie showing that such design was copied from such work.

(g) REPRODUCTION FOR TEACHING OR ANALYSIS—It is not an infringement of the exclusive rights of a design owner for a person to reproduce the design in a useful article or in any other form solely for the purpose of teaching, analyzing, or evaluating the appearance, concepts, or techniques embodied in the design, or the function of the useful article embodying the design.

10. Sec. 1310. Application for registration:

(a) TIME LIMIT FOR APPLICATION FOR REGISTRATION—Protection under this chapter shall be lost if application for registration of the design is not made within 2 years after the date on which the design is first made public.

(b) WHEN DESIGN IS MADE PUBLIC—A design is made public when an existing useful article embodying the design is anywhere publicly exhibited, publicly distributed, or offered for sale or sold to the public by the owner of the design or with the owner's consent.

(c) APPLICATION BY OWNER OF DESIGN—Application for registration may be made by the owner of the design.

(d) CONTENTS OF APPLICATION—The application for registration shall be made to the Administrator and shall state:

(1) the name and address of the designer or designers of the design;

(2) the name and address of the owner if different from the designer;

(3) the specific name of the useful article embodying the design;

(4) the date, if any, that the design was first made public, if such date was earlier than the date of the application;

(5) affirmation that the design has been fixed in a useful article; and

(6) such other information as may be required by the Administrator.

The application for registration may include a description setting forth the salient features of the design, but the absence of such a description shall not prevent registration under this chapter.

(e) SWORN STATEMENT—The application for registration shall be accompanied by a statement under oath by the applicant or the applicant's duly authorized agent or representative, setting forth, to the best of the applicant's knowledge and belief:

(1) that the design is original and was created by the designer or designers named in the application;

(2) that the design has not previously been registered on behalf of the applicant or the applicant's predecessor in title; and

(3) that the applicant is the person entitled to protection and to registration under this chapter.

If the design has been made public with the design notice prescribed in section 1306, the statement shall also describe the exact form and position of the design notice.

(f) EFFECT OF ERRORS— (1) Error in any statement or assertion as to the utility of the useful article named in the application under this section, the design of which is sought to be registered, shall not affect the protection secured under this chapter.

(2) Errors in omitting a joint designer or in naming an alleged joint designer shall not affect the validity of the registration, or the actual ownership or the protection of the design, unless it is shown that the error occurred with deceptive intent.

(g) DESIGN MADE IN SCOPE OF EMPLOYMENT—In a case in which the design was made within the regular scope of the designer's employment and individual authorship of the design is difficult or impossible to ascribe and the application so states, the name and address of the employer for whom the design was made may be stated instead of that of the individual designer.

(h) PICTORIAL REPRESENTATION OF DESIGN—The application for registration shall be accompanied by two copies of a drawing or other pictorial representation of the useful article embodying the design, having one or more views, adequate to show the design, in a form and style suitable for reproduction, which shall be deemed a part of the application.

(i) DESIGN IN MORE THAN ONE USEFUL ARTICLE—If the distinguishing elements of a design are in substantially the same form in different useful articles, the design shall be protected as to all such useful articles when protected as to one of them, but not more than one registration shall be required for the design.

(j) APPLICATION FOR MORE THAN ONE DESIGN—More than one design may be included in the same application under such conditions as may be prescribed by the Administrator. For each design included in an application the fee prescribed for a single design shall be paid.

11. Sec. 1311. Benefit of earlier filing date in foreign country:

An application for registration of a design filed in the United States by any person who has, or whose legal representative or predecessor or successor in title has, previously filed an application for registration of the same design in a foreign country which extends to designs of owners who are citizens of the United States, or to applications filed under this chapter, similar protection to that provided under this chapter shall have that same effect as if filed in the United States on the date on which the application was first filed in such foreign country, if the application in the United States is filed within 6 months after the earliest date on which any such foreign application was filed.

12. Sec. 1312. Oaths and acknowledgments:

(a) IN GENERAL—Oaths and acknowledgments required by this chapter:

(1) may be made:

(A) before any person in the United States authorized by law to administer oaths; or

(B) when made in a foreign country, before any diplomatic or consular officer of the United States authorized to administer oaths, or before any official authorized to administer oaths in the foreign country concerned, whose authority shall be proved by a certificate of a diplomatic or consular officer of the United States; and

(2) shall be valid if they comply with the laws of the State or country where made.

(b) WRITTEN DECLARATION IN LIEU OF OATH— (1) The Administrator may by rule prescribe that any document which is to be filed under this chapter in the Office of the Administrator and which is required by any law, rule, or other regulation to be under oath, may be subscribed to by a written declaration in such form as the Administrator may prescribe, and such declaration shall be in lieu of the oath otherwise required.

(2) Whenever a written declaration under paragraph (1) is used, the document containing the declaration shall state that willful false statements are punishable by fine or imprisonment, or both, pursuant to section 1001 of title 18, and may jeopardize the validity of the application or document or a registration resulting therefrom.

13. Sec. 1313. Examination of application and issue or refusal of registration:

(a) DETERMINATION OF REGISTRABILITY OF DESIGN; REGISTRATION—Upon the filing of an application for registration in proper form under section 1310, and upon payment of the fee prescribed under section 1316, the Administrator shall determine whether or not the application relates to a design which on its face appears to be subject to protection under this chapter, and, if so, the Register shall register the design. Registration under this subsection shall be announced by publication. The date of registration shall be the date of publication.

(b) REFUSAL TO REGISTER; RECONSIDERATION—If, in the judgment of the Administrator, the application for registration relates to a design which on its face is not subject to protection under this chapter, the Administrator shall send to the applicant a notice of refusal to register and the grounds for the refusal. Within 3 months after the date on which the notice of refusal is sent, the applicant may, by written request, seek reconsideration of the application. After consideration of such a request, the Administrator shall either register the design or send to the applicant a notice of final refusal to register.

(c) APPLICATION TO CANCEL REGISTRATION—Any person who believes he or she is or will be damaged by a registration under this chapter may, upon payment of the prescribed fee, apply to the Administrator at any time to cancel the registration on the ground that the design is not subject to protection under this chapter, stating the reasons for the request. Upon receipt of an application for cancellation, the Administrator shall send to the owner of the design, as shown in the records of the Office of the Administrator, a notice of the application, and the owner shall have a period of 3 months after the date on which such notice is mailed in which to present arguments to the Administrator for support of the validity of the registration. The Administrator shall also have the authority to establish, by regulation, conditions under which the opposing parties may appear and be heard in support of their arguments. If, after the periods provided for the presentation of arguments have expired, the Administrator determines that the applicant for cancellation has established that the design is not subject to protection under this chapter, the Administrator shall order the registration stricken from the record. Cancellation under this subsection shall be announced by publication, and notice of the Administrator's final determination with respect to any application for cancellation shall be sent to the applicant and to the owner of record.

14. Sec. 1314. Certification of registration:

Certificates of registration shall be issued in the name of the United States under the seal of the Office of the Administrator and shall be recorded in the official records of the Office. The certificate shall state the name of the useful article, the date of filing of the application, the date of registration, and the date the design was made public, if earlier than the date of filing of the application, and shall contain a reproduction of the drawing or other pictorial representation of the design. If a description of the salient features of the design appears in the application, the description shall also appear in the certificate. A certificate of registration shall be admitted in any court as prima facie evidence of the facts stated in the certificate.

15.   Sec. 1315. Publication of announcements and indexes:

(a) PUBLICATIONS OF THE ADMINISTRATOR—The Administrator shall publish lists and indexes of registered designs and cancellations of designs and may also publish the drawings or other pictorial representations of registered designs for sale or other distribution.

(b) FILE OF REPRESENTATIVES OF REGISTERED DESIGNS—The Administrator shall establish and maintain a file of the drawings or other pictorial representations of registered designs. The file shall be available for use by the public under such conditions as the Administrator may prescribe.

16.   Sec. 1316. Fees:

The Administrator shall by regulation set reasonable fees for the filing of applications to register designs under this chapter and for other services relating to the administration of this chapter, taking into consideration the cost of providing these services and the benefit of a public record.

17.   Sec. 1317. Regulations:

The Administrator may establish regulations for the administration of this chapter.

18.   Sec. 1318. Copies of records:

Upon payment of the prescribed fee, any person may obtain a certified copy of any official record of the Office of the Administrator that relates to this chapter. That copy shall be admissible in evidence with the same effect as the original.

19.   Sec. 1319. Correction of errors in certificates:

The Administrator may, by a certificate of correction under seal, correct any error in a registration incurred through the fault of the Office, or, upon payment of the required fee, any error of a clerical or typographical nature occurring in good faith but not through the fault of the Office. Such registration, together with the certificate, shall thereafter have the same effect as if it had been originally issued in such corrected form.

20. Sec. 1320. Ownership and transfer:

(a) PROPERTY RIGHT IN DESIGN—The property right in a design subject to protection under this chapter shall vest in the designer, the legal representatives of a deceased designer or of one under legal incapacity, the employer for whom the designer created the design in the case of a design made within the regular scope of the designer's employment, or a person to whom the rights of the designer or of such employer have been transferred. The person in whom the property right is vested shall be considered the owner of the design.

(b) TRANSFER OF PROPERTY RIGHT—The property right in a registered design, or a design for which an application for registration has been or may be filed, may be assigned, granted, conveyed, or mortgaged by an instrument in writing, signed by the owner, or may be bequeathed by will.

(c) OATH OR ACKNOWLEDGEMENT OF TRANSFER—An oath or acknowledgment under section 1312 shall be prima facie evidence of the execution of an assignment, grant, conveyance, or mortgage under subsection (b).

(d) RECORDATION OF TRANSFER—An assignment, grant, conveyance, or mortgage under subsection (b) shall be void as against any subsequent purchaser or mortgagee for a valuable consideration, unless it is recorded in the Office of the Administrator within 3 months after its date of execution or before the date of such subsequent purchase or mortgage.

21. Sec. 1321. Remedy for infringement:

(a) IN GENERAL—The owner of a design is entitled, after issuance of a certificate of registration of the design under this chapter, to institute an action for any infringement of the design.

(b) REVIEW OF REFUSAL TO REGISTER— (1) Subject to paragraph (2), the owner of a design may seek judicial review of a final refusal of the Administrator to register the design under this chapter by bringing a civil action, and may in the same action, if the court adjudges the design subject to protection under this chapter, enforce the rights in that design under this chapter.

(2) The owner of a design may seek judicial review under this section if:

(A) the owner has previously duly filed and prosecuted to final refusal an application in proper form for registration of the design;

(B) the owner causes a copy of the complaint in the action to be delivered to the Administrator within 10 days after the commencement of the action; and

(C) the defendant has committed acts in respect to the design which would constitute infringement with respect to a design protected under this chapter.

(c) ADMINISTRATOR AS PARTY TO ACTION—The Administrator may, at the Administrator's option, become a party to the action with respect to the issue of registrability of the design claim by entering an appearance within 60 days after being served with the complaint, but the failure of the Administrator to become a party shall not deprive the court of jurisdiction to determine that issue.

(d) USE OF ARBITRATION TO RESOLVE DISPUTE—The parties to an infringement dispute under this chapter, within such time as may be specified by the Administrator by regulation, may determine the dispute, or any aspect of the dispute, by arbitration. Arbitration shall be governed by title 9. The parties shall give notice of any arbitration award to the Administrator, and such award shall, as between the parties to the arbitration, be dispositive of the issues to which it relates. The arbitration award shall be unenforceable until such notice is given. Nothing in this subsection shall preclude the Administrator from determining whether a design is subject to registration in a cancellation proceeding under section 1313(c).

22. Sec. 1322. Injunctions:

(a) IN GENERAL—A court having jurisdiction over actions under this chapter may grant injunctions in accordance with the principles of equity to prevent infringement of a design under this chapter, including, in its discretion, prompt relief by temporary restraining orders and preliminary injunctions.

(b) DAMAGES FOR INJUNCTIVE RELIEF WRONGFULLY OBTAINED—A seller or distributor who suffers damage by reason of injunctive relief wrongfully obtained under this section has a cause of action against the applicant for such injunctive relief and may recover such relief as may be appropriate, including damages for lost profits, cost of materials, loss of good will, and punitive damages in instances where the injunctive relief was sought in bad faith, and, unless the court finds extenuating circumstances, reasonable attorney's fees.

23. Sec. 1323. Recovery for infringement:

(a) DAMAGES—Upon a finding for the claimant in an action for infringement under this chapter, the court shall award the claimant damages adequate to compensate for the infringement. In addition, the court may increase the damages to such amount, not exceeding $50,000 or $1 per copy, whichever is greater, as the court determines to be just. The damages awarded shall constitute compensation and not a penalty. The court may receive expert testimony as an aid to the determination of damages.

(b) INFRINGER'S PROFITS—As an alternative to the remedies provided in subsection (a), the court may award the claimant the infringer's profits resulting from the sale of the copies if the court finds that the infringer's sales are reasonably related to the use of the claimant's design. In such a case, the claimant shall be required to prove only the amount of the infringer's sales and the infringer shall be required to prove its expenses against such sales.

(c) STATUTE OF LIMITATIONS—No recovery under subsection (a) or (b) shall be had for any infringement committed more than 3 years before the date on which the complaint is filed.

(d) ATTORNEY'S FEES—In an action for infringement under this chapter, the court may award reasonable attorney's fees to the prevailing party.

(e) DISPOSITION OF INFRINGING AND OTHER ARTICLES—The court may order that all infringing articles, and any plates, molds, patterns, models, or other means specifically adapted for making the articles, be delivered up for destruction or other disposition as the court may direct.

24. Sec. 1324. Power of court over registration:

In any action involving the protection of a design under this chapter, the court, when appropriate, may order registration of a design under this chapter or the cancellation of such a registration. Any such order shall be certified by the court to the Administrator, who shall make an appropriate entry upon the record.

25. Sec. 1325. Liability for action on registration fraudulently obtained:

Any person who brings an action for infringement knowing that registration of the design was obtained by a false or fraudulent representation materially affecting the rights under this chapter, shall be liable in the sum of $10,000, or such part of that amount as the court may determine. That amount shall be to compensate the defendant and shall be charged against the plaintiff and paid to the defendant, in addition to such costs and attorney's fees of the defendant as may be assessed by the court.

26. Sec. 1326. Penalty for false marking:

(a) IN GENERAL—Whoever, for the purpose of deceiving the public, marks upon, applies to, or uses in advertising in connection with an article made, used, distributed, or sold, a design which is not protected under this chapter, a design notice specified in section 1306, or any other words or symbols importing that the design is protected under this chapter, knowing that the design is not so protected, shall pay a civil fine of not more than $500 for each such offense.

(b) SUIT BY PRIVATE PERSONS—Any person may sue for the penalty established by subsection (a), in which event one-half of the penalty shall be awarded to the person suing and the remainder shall be awarded to the United States.

27. Sec. 1327. Penalty for false representation:

Whoever knowingly makes a false representation materially affecting the rights obtainable under this chapter for the purpose of obtaining registration of a design under this chapter shall pay a penalty of not less than $500 and not more than $1,000, and any rights or privileges that individual may have in the design under this chapter shall be forfeited.

28. Sec. 1328. Enforcement by Treasury and Postal Service:

(a) REGULATIONS—The Secretary of the Treasury and the United States Postal Service shall separately or jointly issue regulations for the enforcement of the rights set forth in section 1308 with respect to importation. Such regulations may require, as a condition for the exclusion of articles from the United States, that the person seeking exclusion take any one or more of the following actions:

(1) Obtain a court order enjoining, or an order of the International Trade Commission under section 337 of the Tariff Act of 1930 excluding, importation of the articles.

(2) Furnish proof that the design involved is protected under this chapter and that the importation of the articles would infringe the rights in the design under this chapter.

(3) Post a surety bond for any injury that may result if the detention or exclusion of the articles proves to be unjustified.

(b) SEIZURE AND FORFEITURE—Articles imported in violation of the rights set forth in section 1308 are subject to seizure and forfeiture in the same manner as property imported in violation of the customs laws. Any such forfeited articles shall be destroyed as directed by the Secretary of the Treasury or the court, as the case may be, except that the articles may be returned to the country of export whenever it is shown to the satisfaction of the Secretary of the Treasury that the importer had no reasonable grounds for believing that his or her acts constituted a violation of the law.

29. Sec. 1329. Relation to design patent law:

The issuance of a design patent under title 35, United States Code, for an original design for an article of manufacture shall terminate any protection of the original design under this chapter.

30. Sec. 1330. Common law and other rights unaffected:

Nothing in this chapter shall annul or limit:

(1) common law or other rights or remedies, if any, available to or held by any person with respect to a design which has not been registered under this chapter; or

(2) any right under the trademark laws or any right protected against unfair competition.

31. Sec. 1331. Administrator; Office of the Administrator:

In this chapter, the 'Administrator' is the Register of Copyrights, and the 'Office of the Administrator' and the 'Office' refer to the Copyright Office of the Library of Congress.

32. Sec. 1332. No retroactive effect:

Protection under this chapter shall not be available for any design that has been made public under section 1310(b) before the effective date of this chapter.'

4. SEC. 503. CONFORMING AMENDMENTS.

(a) TABLE OF CHAPTERS—The table of chapters for title 17, United States Code, is amended by adding at the end the following:

1301.

(b) JURISDICTION OF DISTRICT COURTS OVER DESIGN ACTIONS- (1) Section 1338(c) of title 28, United States Code, is amended by inserting ', and to exclusive rights in designs under chapter 13 of title 17,' after 'title 17'.

(2)(A) The section heading for section 1338 of title 28, United States Code, is amended by inserting '**designs,**' after '**mask works;**'

(B) The item relating to section 1338 in the table of sections at the beginning of chapter 85 of title 28, United States Code, is amended by inserting 'designs,' after 'mask works;'

(c) PLACE FOR BRINGING DESIGN ACTIONS—(1) Section 1400(a) of title 28, United States Code, is amended by inserting 'or designs' after 'mask works.'

(2) The section heading for section 1400 of title 28, United States Code, is amended to read as follows:

1. Patents and copyrights, mask works, and designs.

(3) The item relating to section 1400 in the table of sections at the beginning of chapter 87 of title 28, United States Code, is amended to read as follows:

1400. Patents and copyrights, mask works, and designs.'

(d) ACTIONS AGAINST THE UNITED STATES—Section 1498(e) of title 28, United States Code, is amended by inserting ', and to exclusive rights in designs under chapter 13 of title 17,' after 'title 17.'

5. SEC. 504. JOINT STUDY OF THE EFFECT OF THIS TITLE.

(a) IN GENERAL—Not later than 1 year after the date of the enactment of this Act, and not later than 2 years after such date of enactment, the Register of Copyrights and the Commissioner of Patents and Trademarks shall submit to the Committees on the Judiciary of the Senate and the House of Representatives a joint report evaluating the effect of the amendments made by this title.

(b) ELEMENTS FOR CONSIDERATION—In carrying out subsection (a), the Register of Copyrights and the Commissioner of Patents and Trademarks shall consider:

(1) the extent to which the amendments made by this title has been effective in suppressing infringement of the design of vessel hulls;

(2) the extent to which the registration provided for in chapter 13 of title 17, United States Code, as added by this title, has been utilized;

(3) the extent to which the creation of new designs of vessel hulls have been encouraged by the amendments made by this title;

(4) the effect, if any, of the amendments made by this title on the price of vessels with hulls protected under such amendments; and

(5) such other considerations as the Register and the Commissioner may deem relevant to accomplish the purposes of the evaluation conducted under subsection (a).

6. SEC. 505. EFFECTIVE DATE.

The amendments made by sections 502 and 503 shall take effect on the date of the enactment of this Act and shall remain in effect until the end of the 2-year period beginning on such date of enactment. No cause of action based on chapter 13 of title 17, United States Code, as added by this title, may be filed after the end of that 2-year period.

Speaker of the House of Representatives.
Vice President of the United States and
President of the Senate.

Endnotes

Chapter 1

1. imdb.com
2. http://graphics.stanford.edu/~dk/google_name_origin.html
3. http://www.inc.com/magazine/20070601/features-how-to-kill-a-great-idea.html
4. http://myspade.com/
5. http://en.wikipedia.org/wiki/Myspace
6. http://www.inc.com/magazine/20070601/features-how-to-kill-a-great-idea.html
7. http://www.consumerreports.org/cro/magazine-archive/2011/june/electronics-computers/state-of-the-net/facebook-concerns/index.htm
8. http://en.wikipedia.org/wiki/Facebook
9. Ibid.
10. Ibid.
11. http://en.wikipedia.org/wiki/Myspace
12. http://en.wikipedia.org/wiki/Web_2.0
13. http://en.wikipedia.org/wiki/Twitter
14. AP 10/5/2009

Chapter 2

15. http://www.thesmokinggun.com/documents/florida/girls-busted-phony-facebook-pages
16. ISBN 978-0-4701-9082-1

Chapter 3

17. http://www.rcfp.org/news/mag/26-3/sct-thenewna.html
18. http://itlaw.wikia.com/wiki/Falwell_v._Cohn Foot Note
19. http://blogs.wsj.com/deals/2010/12/22/439-ways-to-hate-bank-of-america

Chapter 4
20. http://chris.pirillo.com/how-long-should-yahoo-google-or-microsoft-keep-your-personal-data

21. http://www.mediapost.com/publications/?fa=Articles.showArticle&art_aid=146493

22. http://www.bruceclay.com/blog/2006/03/no-email-is-safe/

Chapter 5
23. Under Section 512(f) of the Copyright Act one who knowingly materially misrepresents a claim of infringement is liable for any damages, including costs and attorneys' fees, incurred by the alleged infringer or ISP injured by the misrepresentation, as the result of the service provider relying upon the misrepresentation in removing or disabling access to the material or activity claimed to be infringing. http://www.chillingeffects.org/question.cgi?QuestionID=858

Chapter 6
24. http://sunlightfoundation.com/

25. See Appendix Two.

Chapter 9
26. http://sportsillustrated.asia/vault/article/magazine/MAG1185398/index.htm

Chapter 10
27. http://www.techdirt.com/articles/20091229/1649017538.shtml

28. http://www.internetcommercelaw.com/2010/01/articles/communications-decency-act/nemet-chevrolet-v-consumeraffairscom-4th-circuit-reaffirms-its-position-that-the-communications-decency-act-provides-immunity-from-the-burden-of-defending-a-lawsuit/

Acknowledgements

In appreciating those who have walked the journey with me, I must start with Barbara. You have been the better half of my whole; my lover, friend and business partner. The things that have brought satisfaction in my life both professionally and personally all trace their roots back to you.

To Aaron, my "go to" guy—doing hand-to-hand combat with algorithms, indexing and employee management on a daily basis. The exploitation of good people has guaranteed you a permanent vocation until you fall over!

Jeremy, thanks for jumping on the train and adding your perspective, counsel and humor. You are indeed a writer in your own right.

Kurt—we have discovered that there can be lemonade created from every bitter fruit when there is the sweetness of friendship and enough pressure is applied. Ten years in the squeeze is enough. Consider this your glass; full, chilled, bitter and yet just a little bit sweet.

Every man should have a support system walking through life and I am no exception. Thanks to my friends Glenn Simmons, Rob Frazier, Thaddeus Heffner, Jim Gibson and Pastor Stan Mitchell and my family at GracePointe Church in Franklin, Tennessee. They all knowingly or unknowingly contributed to this book as they stood by me while I was *Violated Online.*

Many thanks to my friend Tom Nelson for not enabling me so that I could take the quick path, and to Doug Dawson for being an encouragement and for showing me that this book made cents.

My publisher, David Dunham, has been patient, has listened, learned and has encouraged me as I navigated my way into being a freshman writer. Now the fun begins.

I must also end with Barbara; years from now we will look back on this journey and wonder how we walked through all of it. For me, I know that *Everything Belongs*. To God be the glory.

About the Author

Steven Wyer's career as a businessman and entrepreneur has spanned more than thirty years. Wyer has founded companies that provided services to the nation's largest financial institutions, managed almost a billion dollars of consumer debt and been recognized as a visionary within several industries. He has fought the Securities Exchange Commission for almost a decade over charges leveled against him. These unfounded allegations made their way to the Internet and profoundly impacted his professional and personal life. Since then Mr. Wyer has discovered that he is not alone . . . that there are millions of other individuals that have been violated online.

As the Managing Director of Reputation Advocate, Steven Wyer now helps professionals and businesses worldwide reclaim their reputations and credibility. Mr. Wyer lives a contented life in Franklin, Tennessee with his wife, his children, and a dog and a cat.

Author photo: Steve Herlihy

Jeremy Dunlap is a nationally recognized writer, trainer and speaker. Mr. Dunlap works with the Baker Communications core facilitative team. His clients include NASA, Dell, the United States Army, Navy, Marine Corp and Air Force, as well as Naval Special Forces. When not traveling, he invests his time with his family in Nashville, Tennessee.

For more information on Search Engine Reputation Management contact:

Reputation Advocate
2550 Meridian Blvd. Suite 350
Franklin, TN 37067
888-229-0746
ReputationAdvocate.com

Violated Online
P.O. Box 549
Franklin, TN 37067
ViolatedOnline.com